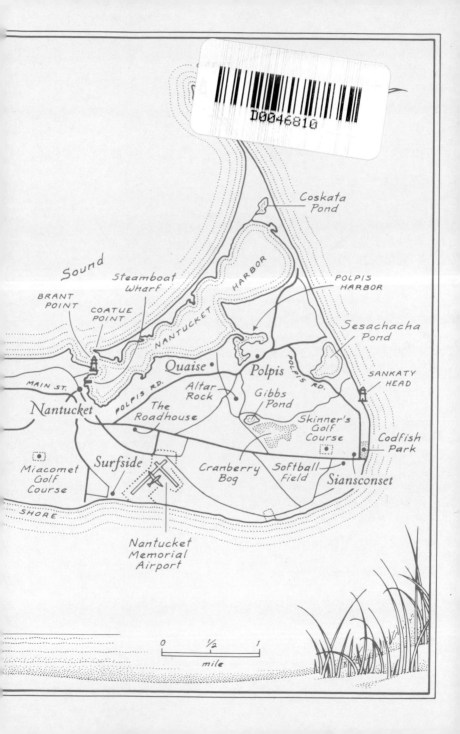

Time and Tide

ALSO IN THE CROWN JOURNEYS SERIES

Time and Tide

A WALK THROUGH NANTUCKET

Frank Conroy

*To Beo and George,
On the occasion of
Christmas, 2010.
Love,
Debbie and Jim Quick*

▟ CROWN JOURNEYS

CROWN PUBLISHERS · NEW YORK

Copyright © 2004 by Frank Conroy

Published by Crown Publishers, New York, New York.
Member of the Crown Publishing Group, a division of Random House, Inc.
www.crownpublishing.com

CROWN JOURNEYS and the Crown Journeys colophon are registered
trademarks of Random House, Inc.

Printed in the United States of America

Design by Lauren Dong

Map by Jackie Aher

Library of Congress Cataloging-in-Publication Data
Conroy, Frank, 1936–
Time and tide: a walk through Nantucket / Frank Conroy.
(Crown Journeys series)
1. Nantucket Island (Mass.)—Description and travel.   2. Walking—
Massachusettes—Nantucket Island.   I. Title.   II. Series.
F72.N2C66   2004
974.4'97043—dc22   2003020317

ISBN 1-4000-4659-9

10 9 8 7 6 5 4 3 2 1

First Edition

To Liam

CONTENTS

Contents

PHOTOGRAPHS

Time and Tide

PREFACE

I HAVE WRITTEN BEFORE ABOUT MY EARLIEST
memory, but since it involves Nantucket, I'll do it
again. I was perhaps three years old, being held by
someone so I could look over the railing of the huge
ferryboat on which we were passengers, to see the
wharf, the water below, and the boys from town diving for coins thrown down by the people around us.
Today, in my mind's eye I can still see the images, the
moving images, although as if through a tube, images
in a bright circle, all else—the larger setting, the boat,
the town, the sky—lost.

A flashing coin is thrown, three or four boys dive,
almost simultaneously, into the green water and disappear for a while. Almost simultaneously they emerge,
one of them holding the coin aloft before slipping
it in his cheek and looking up for the next nickel
or dime. Young as I was I admired the boys, envy-

ing their energy and deft swimming. They seemed cheerful but also slightly tough, which interested me. The memory ends.

It was the Steamboat Wharf of Nantucket, I learned many years later and the occasion, a family excursion to an old hotel in Siasconset noted for its artsy clientele. (The building was torn down years ago and is forgotten now.)

I grew up with this isolated memory without knowing where it had occurred. I did not find out until I was in my thirties, when my mother mentioned it one night, apropos of nothing in particular, from what would turn out to be her deathbed in a New York City hospital.

Busy Days/Hot Nights

*I*N 1955, AT THE AGE OF NINETEEN, I ARRIVED
on Nantucket for what I thought was the first time,
accompanied by my college girlfriend and two other
Haverford/Bryn Mawr couples. All six of us rented a
three-room apartment over a bicycle shop (which still
stands) for the summer. Those of us who needed
them got jobs fairly quickly, because even in those
days Nantucket in summer relied on imported labor.
We'd come on a whim, the way kids used to do in the
Eisenhower years, confident that we'd survive one
way or another. My girlfriend got a job as the hostess
of a small restaurant, I played the piano at the Whaler's
Lounge in the basement of a ramshackle wooden
hotel run by the Manchester family (where now
stands the Jared Coffin House, a brick nineteenth-
century building, still a hotel, pricey, with nothing
ramshackle about it). One of the guys boned up on

the small island's history from sources provided by a touring outfit and met the morning ferry every day to hawk the day-trippers into sightseeing rides in his little bus. A couple of the girls waited tables in a seafood joint. We survived, and had fun, walking the miles of empty beaches on our off time, swimming, having cookouts. We didn't use the apartment for anything but sleep, so jammed in were we those hot nights. Busy kids.

NANTUCKET IS AN island, roughly thirty miles out to sea, and its shape is important for several reasons. It has been described as a crescent moon by one writer, but to me it looks like some fantasized elf's slipper— Madaket Harbor a worn-away toe, Surfside the sole, Siasconset the heel, Wauwinet the top of the heel, with a strip running up higher to Coskata, the long strip down Coatue, where the slipper's laces would tie, and then, even higher above Coskata, the final decorative tassel of Great Point.

The island itself is about fourteen miles long, and averages out at perhaps four miles wide, except for the long eastern shore, less than half of which is habitable. The sandy beach just north of Siasconset (or 'Sconset, as it is called by islanders) is the easternmost edge of the United States. The familiar Mercator Projection to be seen in every schoolroom makes it look like Maine sticks out farther, but that is no more than an effect of flattening three dimensions into two. On a globe Nantucket beats Maine by between two and three degrees.

As you look at a map of Nantucket, notice the small points of Coatue jutting into Nantucket Harbor. (They are named First Point, Second Point, Third Point, Five Fingered Point, Bass Point, and Wyers Point.) Nantucket Harbor is in fact a series of basins, spilling sequentially one into the other as the tide rises or falls. The circular movement of the water within the basins cutting and shaping the thin, grassy strip into the configurations revealed on the map.

The harbor is five miles long, and is of special interest to marine scientists and geographers because its basin arrangement, and the way the water moves in circles within it, are unique in the world. I have personally explored every part of the harbor with a series (over thirty-five years) of small boats, and bear witness to its beauty. The sudden, slightly exotic atmosphere of Coskata at the head of the harbor, inaccessible except by water, usually deserted, except in August, with its glades, hills, long ponds, and dunes, is especially alluring. Any one of the points, as you return, is worth exploring. You can swim in the shallows, fish for bass or bluefish in deeper waters, or simply cruise along in the sun.

Despite its great area one is never out of sight of land in the harbor, which is reassuring to the inexperienced sailor. If a fog bank rolls in and you can't see more than twenty feet in any direction, the thing to do is cut your engines, or lower your sail, and wait it out.

As seen from the Atlantic Ocean, Melville describes Nantucket thusly: "a mere hillock, and elbow of sand; all beach, without a background."

And so it still appears from a distance, although not quite as bare as it was in the first half of the nineteenth century. A sense of the ocean—the sound of it, or the smell of it, or a certain purity to the air—is felt everywhere on the island. Indeed, it's a pretty small patch of land, mostly moors because the severity of the winter winds preclude the growth of trees over much of its surface. There are a few "hidden forests" where the topography allows mostly scrub oaks. It resembles southern Scotland more than it does the neighboring island of Martha's Vineyard or the mainland. It is best explored on foot, off the roads, in September and October, when the moors change colors, veering toward purple, and the sunlight turns winey. Some find it too bleak, but many, like myself, do not.

~~~

BUSY KIDS, WORKING, making love, endlessly talking and arguing about the books and ideas we'd been exposed to the previous winter, we didn't have much time to explore. We seemed unable to get out of the lower Main Street area, with its side streets, post office, drug store, five & ten, etc.—that fifth of the town that had been destroyed by the Great Fire of 1846 (which was the final blow to the island's foundering whaling industry) and rebuilt despite hard financial times. Once in a while we'd bike out to Surfside, or walk around the crumbling wharfs and slips of the town waterfront, but that was about it. Not even the boy driving the tour bus saw very much going out to 'Sconset and back, stopping every now and then for water views or a look at the cranberry bogs. What one saw from the roads represented only a hint of the uniqueness of the island in those days. Now, with so many houses, hedges, landscaping, fences, and general prettifying on the sides of the roads, the hint is a good deal weaker.

But much of the town of Nantucket looks a lot like it did fifty years ago. The lower part, where we roamed as kids, is similar to what the day-trippers see now, although the shops are more densely commercialized, and the prices are ridiculously high.

What we did not see then, and surprisingly few off islanders are aware of now, is that part of town that survived the fire: an entirely residential area on Upper Main Street and off Upper Main Street with a maze of lanes, narrow streets, alleys, and paths. To walk through old Nantucket town is to enter a living dream of the past—a hundred and fifty, sixty, seventy years ago, sometimes two hundred years ago, these beautiful houses were built. Federalist, Greek Revival, and Quaker architecture predominate. In terms of the size of the streets, lanes, buildings, narrow sidewalks, and especially the harmonious proportions of it all, it is as it was. It is not a museum, people live here, but as quiet, calm, and peaceful as anyone could wish. One finds oneself walking softly, talking softly, without consciously deciding to do so. I have visited and seen many lovely towns across America, but nothing has taken my breath away like old Nantucket.

How did it come about? First, Nantucket was once a place in which the rich were truly, mind-bogglingly rich. I don't mean now, I mean in the first half of the nineteenth century, when whaling ships would go out to the Pacific Ocean for a couple of years and return to home port in Nantucket with a million dollars' worth of oil belowdecks for their owners. There was a working class in Nantucket, to be sure. Coopers, blacksmiths, carpenters, sailors, clam diggers, etc., who lived mostly on the low ground, near the water. Up a bit higher, on Orange Street, for instance, ship's captains built solid houses with widow's walks on the roofs from which one could see what was happening in the harbor (or put out a chimney fire). The filthy rich—boat owners, investors, and businessmen—built fine expensive homes on the high ground behind the Pacific National Bank at the top of Main Street. There was a certain amount of showing off on Upper Main, a kind of architectural one-upmanship in terms of size, style, and artistic discernment—in perfect taste, of course. Nothing vulgar.

But then things changed. As Clay Lancaster explains in *Nantucket in the Nineteenth Century,* "The island's chief industry—whale oil—had been reduced to half by the introduction of camphine; it was cut another thirty percent by lard oil, and finally was given the death blow by the production of kerosene from petroleum and by piped gas." The great whaling ships became passenger ships carrying prospectors (including a large part of the working class from Nantucket) out to California in the Gold Rush of '49 on a one-way trip for ships and passengers alike.

Well, there was still sheep herding. The animals had enjoyed more or less the run of the island for a long time, stripping vegetation efficiently (hence Melville's description), the cranberry industry was creeping along, as well as the extremely fragile beginnings of tourism, but the big money was gone. Hard times, even on Upper Main, where no one could do more than basic upkeep, and sometimes not even that, of the formerly grand houses. Many were boarded up. Even into the twentieth century they remained unimproved, untouched except for the most basic and superficial attentions. A ghostly neighborhood, sunk in the amber of a financial depression. Bad luck then, but good luck for us. Rich people came back eventually, more than a hundred years later, and they recognized the architectural gems as worth saving. They restored. They did not remodel, rebuild, modernize, tear down, or replace, as was going on in the rest of America. Over time they restored the whole neighborhood, and even extended it slightly with tasteful new structures in harmony with the old. The result constitutes an authentic treasure—an unforgettable architectural experience for even the most jaded.

⚋

ROBERT MOONEY, AN island attorney, in his interesting source book *Nantucket Only Yesterday,* begins his sixth chapter with the following: "The decade of the fifties marked a turning point from the long tradition of shared interests and close relationships within the Nantucket community. Prior to those years, the center of town was the place both residents and summer visitors mingled for shopping and recreational pursuits, typified by the evening sing-a-longs on Main Street after which everyone went home at ten o'clock."

There is no doubt much truth in this view, and certainly one's impulse is to defer to Mr. Mooney, an extremely knowledgeable man about his hometown, but I think the larger turning point was in the seventies, and then again, even larger, in the nineties. Mooney believes, "The influx of tourists from the Hyannis boats . . . [and] the direct air service from Boston and New York brought a younger and livelier crowd . . ." And it doubtless did, but the really big changes were to come later.

In the fifties there were the town of Nantucket, the village of Siasconset, and the beach at Surfside. Everything happened in those three locations. The rest was moors, ponds, open space, and occasionally a house off Polpis Road, or a small cluster of houses near the water in a place like Quidnet, Polpis, or Wauwinet. (This last had a wonderful quiet old wooden hotel favored by the late John Cheever.) But the action, such as it was, was in lower Nantucket. The year-round population of the island had remained fairly steady for a hundred years at about 3,500. Mr. Mooney, who was in their number, describes their anti-Semitic, antigay feelings (which are still there for many year-rounders), suspiciousness of "flashy New Yorkers," and some snobbism about day-trippers. I suppose a certain number of people felt that way, but my sense, arriving in 1955, was that most islanders were genuinely happy to see us. The winters were long, and it must have been stimulating to see some new faces, to feel the pace of life pick up a bit.

Summer people (as opposed to day-trippers) arrived on the large ferries like the *Uncatena* and the *Nobska,* which carried people, automobiles, and semis from Woods Hole on Cape Cod to Nantucket Harbor. As the boats rounded Brant Point through the narrow channel the battered old wharves and piers of the waterfront were suddenly revealed, and up higher, farther back, the church steeples, white and gold in the sun.

It was a town in those days, a real town in which everyone knew everyone else and behaved, perforce, in a civil manner, even toward the "summer people," who outnumbered the year-rounders to be sure, but not so much that some of the civility didn't rub off on them. The small-town "feel" was one of the reasons myself and others kept returning summer after summer. It was a tonic indeed after New York City, where I lived after graduating from college. Nantucket was a small, relaxed oasis in the ocean.

Quiet Days/Quiet Nights

NANTUCKET IS DRENCHED WITH MEMORIES of the whaling days and the nineteenth century. It is sodden, to tell the truth. The high school team is "The Whalers," the Nantucket Historical Association Library is 90 percent nineteenth century, as is the Folger Museum, and this history has been logoized and commercialized by the merchants, the Chamber of Commerce, guest houses, etc., to an excessive degree.

Which is not to say it wasn't an interesting time. With most of the male population at sea, the island was controlled and managed almost exclusively by women. They ran local commerce and dominated politics. It was a highly stratified, nuanced, and complex society in which religious issues roiled, social groups parried one against the other, and sexual forces undoubtedly bubbled under everything. ("Nervous? I will spend the night with thee. 25 cents," ran an ad in the paper. A type of ceramic dildo imported from Asia called "He's at home" was a common domestic item.) Nevertheless money and business were king, and the island hummed. An interesting time for many reasons, yet not, of course, the only interesting time.

～～～

DESPITE MR. MOONEY's remarks about direct air service from Boston and New York, the Nantucket airport in the fifties was small and simple—a kind of shed and two short runways which crossed each other, one running roughly north-south, the other east-west. It was agreed there was no need for a tower or the complicated and expensive business of an instrument landing system, although the island, and that particular part of the island especially, was famous for its dense fogs, which could appear without warning and with remarkable speed. Commercial air service, which had been minimal at best, almost disappeared after 1958, when a Northeast Airlines prop DC ended its scheduled run from New York by crashing in the Friday night darkness before it reached the runway, killing twenty-four people and leaving ten survivors (one of whom, Jack Shea, a lawyer, was a friend of long standing; he survived, but couldn't remember much when they found him crawling around in the moors. Years later, he still couldn't recall the details).

In the sixties the runways were lengthened to accommodate jets, the tower was built, and radar/instrument landing was installed. Eventually it became a modern airport, and both commercial and private flying increased steadily through the years until it was busier in summer than any other airport in Massachusetts, including, at times, Logan in Boston. But I'm getting ahead of myself.

∞

AFTER COLLEGE MY girlfriend and I got married. We lived in New York City, but continued to come to Nantucket every summer for twelve years. (Except once we went to Martha's Vineyard and didn't particularly like it—it lacked the ubiquitous ocean smell, the saltiness, the moors, the simplicity and spareness of its smaller sister, the "faraway island," as the Indians called it.) We had enough money to stay all summer long, and enough so we didn't need jobs. We rented different houses in Nantucket along Polpis Road. There weren't all that many houses out of town in the sixties. Most nights, if you sat out on the porch, let's say, you might see the distant flicker of headlights and hear a car on its way to Pocomo or Quidnet or Wauwinet every hour or so. If Nantucket and 'Sconset were dense, close-packed towns, the rest of the island was mostly bare, sparsely populated, and, as a result, quite private. We relished the quietness, took the children (two little boys) to the South Shore with its dunes and deep white beaches almost every day, and spent the evenings reading. The stars at night were spectacular. The clear air and the lack of ambient light opened up the heavens and seemed to bring them closer. Shooting stars were commonplace all summer long.

An interest in the stars and their movements had been a part of Nantucket's culture for a long time. In the nineteenth century virtually everyone owned a telescope with which to search the ocean for sails, or confirm the names of ships coming into the harbor. The same telescopes could be pointed upward.

> *Aside from the study of astronomy, there is the same enjoyment in a night upon the housetop, with the stars . . . there is the same subdued quiet and grateful seriousness . . .*

So sayeth Maria Mitchell in her diaries, and I felt the same way lying on various lawns with good binoculars, and eventually with a Questar, a compact, highly sophisticated catadioptric telescope I'd borrowed from a movie director I knew.

*My love for astronomy was born on that island . . .
the spirit of the place had also much to do with my
pursuit. In Nantucket people quite generally were
in the habit of observing the heavens, and a sextant
was to be found in almost every house. The landscape
was flat . . .*

Maria's interest in science began with her father's
lessons. She became an expert in the adjustment of
precision chronometers while still a child. As a woman
she discovered a comet and was awarded with a medal
from the King of Denmark. She served as a librarian at
the Atheneum for a salary of $100 a year. She helped
arrange the Lyceum lectures—Thoreau, Agassiz (the
Swiss naturalist and glaciologist), Audubon, Emerson,
and other notables whom she convinced to make the
trip and come 'round Brant Point. Eventually she became a professor of astronomy at Vassar College (at
$800 a year). There exists in Nantucket a Maria
Mitchell Association and Observatory to this day, in
tribute to an authentic hometown heroine.

During the sixties my wife, Patty, our children,
Dan and Will, and of course myself took full advantage of what was still a quiet, calm island. We rarely
went to town, although when we did it was still pleasant to visit the library, go to the bookstore, buy a good
wool sweater at the Nobby Shop for a fair price, have
a drink at the Club Car, or buy a raffle ticket from a

lady at a card table in front of the Catholic church. As the streets became more crowded from one summer to the next, we barely noticed.

Outside of town we could walk for miles over the moors or along beaches without seeing a soul. The South Shore dunes were private enough that the occasional nude sunbather might be startled into grabbing his towel to cover himself when a certain State Motor Vehicle Bureau officer (uniformed and armed in the state of Massachusetts) would appear out of nowhere in a specially accessorized low-flying Piper Cub and shout down from above, "You are under arrest for indecent exposure. Stay where you are." Of course the putative offenders always took off pronto and no one was ever arrested. The local police quite sensibly ignored calls from the plane. This same uniformed individual did not endear himself to the board and members of the Sankaty Head Golf Club when he insisted that every golf cart be fitted with headlights, license plates, and everything else needed to meet state motor vehicle regulations because the carts crossed ten feet of a state road between holes two and three. (The club appealed in court and won.) Nantucket has always had oddballs and characters of one kind or another, and local oral history has not forgotten them.

But as quiet as Nantucket seemed to be, changes were under way. And perhaps the very big changes on

the mainland—e.g., the civil rights movement, foreign wars, "changes in the wind," etc.—made it harder
to appreciate the importance of the gradual takeover
of downtown property by a group of businessmen
with a master plan. They began buying in 1964 and
anticipated a complete restructuring of the waterfront
starting in 1966 with the aim of replacing the dwin-
dling fishing industry activity with an economy based
on tourism, an extensive yacht basin, and downtown
retail outlets to serve the very rich in addition to the
day-trippers. Good-bye to the old Five and Ten, the
Upper Deck (a favorite bar of the locals), the Ocean
House where I'd played piano. (What a gig that had
been! Five college waitresses, all cute, who would
gather 'round the piano at closing time, each with her
one free drink—Brandy Alexander—listening to me
play "Tenderly," "Blues in the Night," "The Little
White Cloud That Cried," or whatever else they re-
quested. Severe temptation, and of course I gave in. I
was nineteen years old and completely girl crazy.)

Sherburne Associates had a plan, and even those
who were against it had to admit it was well executed,
and that off-island money began to flow into the island economy. It was pointless to revile Sherburne, or
Mr. Beineke, the so-called Green Stamp King whose
plan it mostly was, because change was inevitable. The
old piers and wharves were falling to pieces, for instance, literally rotting away. The waterfront was a

danger, and not only to children. Sherburne built a new waterfront, starting with Straight Wharf at the foot of Lower Main, and ending with a huge modern yacht basin with hundreds of slips and all necessary support services. The island of Nantucket, with its open spaces, beautiful and well-protected harbor, architectural treasurers, beaches and salt marshes, was essentially powerless to resist change. And it was a plum. Jet service from New York or Boston in a matter of minutes. Charm. Quaintness. Quiet. The gentle rhythms of small-town life. No one, including Mr. Beineke, could have foreseen what would eventually happen.

Settling In

*I*N THE LATE SIXTIES WE LIVED IN BROOKLYN and I occasionally made money as a "script doctor" for the Hollywood studios. My biggest job was an original script for Paramount. They never made the movie, but I was paid thirty thousand dollars. My wife's uncle gave her a matching gift and we thought about land and a summer house. We had in fact admired a certain large area off Polpis Road called Quaise, almost all of it owned by one man, and had asked him, every year, to remember us if he ever wanted to sell a few acres. Things came together magically—the movie money, the match, and the arrival of the landowner's first son at the gates of an expensive college. We bought a lovely bit of land that contained a mini forest, a beautiful salt marsh behind which could be seen the southern end of Polpis Harbor. We could walk down to the water on our own land. I hired a six-foot-seven-inch bearded back-to-nature M.I.T. engineering graduate to oversee a bunch of hippie carpenters. An architect friend purchased an old tobacco barn in the wilds of western Pennsylvania, dismantled the frame with some help from a nearby hippie commune, figured out how much siding would be needed, had it cut at a sawmill, and brought the whole thing—hand-hewn chestnut beams and raw white oak boards—on a semi which came around Brant Point in late '68. I drew up a design, the architect did the specs and solved the "fenestration" problem, and by the spring of '69 the house was almost finished. And so, unfortunately (to put it mildly, and for reasons that

The Barn going up.

had nothing to do with Nantucket), was my marriage. The divorce was as amicable as I suppose it was possible to be. My wife kept the brownstone in Brooklyn, and I got Nantucket.

Somewhere in his enormous body of work, John Updike writes, if I remember correctly, that the ideal size of a community is five thousand. Nantucket's year-round population was stable, as I said before, for a very long time, but in the early seventies it began to move toward Updike's magic number. It was a different kind of community from the small-town/semi-pastoral atmosphere in which Updike spent his boyhood. You're thirty miles out to sea, for starters. I don't have much nostalgia for Nantucket in the seventies. Personally it was a tough time both emotionally and economically. I was a writer, after all, and, to make it worse, a literary writer. I left Brooklyn with three hundred dollars, no job prospects, and an unheated, unfinished barn on a remote island my only possession.

The population included people who worked for the water company, the telephone company, the town itself, etc., as you would find in any town, and an awful lot of people who served the summer people in one capacity or another, building or taking care of houses, running the hotels and guest houses, and who had to make enough in three and a half months to support themselves for twelve.

In addition there were a lot of odd people, non-conformists, wounded people (like myself), drop-outs, fantasists, hiders from reality, wanderers, loners, weirdos, and characters. It was a kind of halfway house for some, and some never left.

I've already mentioned the man who worked at the State Motor Vehicle Registry office. A thoroughly nasty guy. But then there was Sam, a cheerful, good-hearted simpleton who hung around downtown with his beloved pet rabbit Floppy, and whose Deep South black accent was almost indecipherable, but whose smile was not. He was the town fool, essentially, and the town took care of him. (He never begged, but he got by.) It was a simpler time, as they say.

Perhaps the best-known character was Mildred Jewett, known as Madaket Millie, who was born on the island in 1910 and raised on a small farm on the west end. Her mother had disappeared, her father was ailing, and it was up to her to "work the farm, milk the cows, and spend a lonely life by the sea," as Robert Mooney explains in *Nantucket Only Yesterday*. She was a strange woman, big, ugly, tough, and private. What probably saved her sanity was her connection to the Coast Guard boys at the small Madaket Coast Guard station. "The lonely young sailors took a liking to her, and she ran errands to town for them." World War II provided some excitement. "Millie was the civil defense officer and air raid warden for Madaket, which

she patrolled on a big horse. Woe to the careless cus-
tomer who violated the blackout on Millie's watch."

After the war the station closed, but Millie was
given a plaque for her cottage designating it as the
United States Coast Guard West End Command, and
was officially appointed Chief Officer. She wore the
Coast Guard cap over her wild hair for the rest of her
life. She was no simpleton, and bought up a fishing
shack or two near Hither Creek, renting them out to
young people. In fact Maggie, a twenty-three-year-

Madaket Millie.

old girl from Boston, whom I was eventually to marry, lived in one of Millie's properties. Maggie never saw Millie except to hand over the rent, and although she doesn't like to admit it, the woman scared her. For that matter she scared me.

But the town was proud of her, and protected her. The oral history describes the death of her father, who had been bedridden for years, cared for, cleaned, and fed by Millie alone. When the body was delivered to the hospital it was clear that the old man had been shot in the head. Quite a few nurses and hospital workers must have noticed it, but the doctor on duty was also the medical examiner for the County of Nantucket. He filled out the form, listing the cause of death as heart failure, and signed with a flourish. A brave act, if indeed it happened. The doctor was rather an odd fish himself, with only a partial belief in the science of medicine. He was very cavalier with his patients, including me, one of his friends. I never asked him about the story because I knew I'd never get a straight answer from him, so much did he love affecting an air of mystery.

TAKE ANOTHER LOOK at the map. I lived about halfway between the towns of Nantucket and 'Sconset, off Polpis Road behind the first salt marsh at the south end of the harbor. In those days there were no other houses nearby. I saw a completely different Nantucket when I became a year-rounder, a pretty tight place where it wasn't easy to make a buck. The action in town—the rebuilding of the harbor and other Sherburne projects—was covered by old time local labor. I managed to survive the first winter by doing magazine work by mail, playing the piano in a year-round bar, cashing small royalty checks from my book, and living on the cheap. I installed electric heaters in the bedroom and the kitchen, but the barn hadn't been built with winter in mind and I spent a lot of time in the crawl space underneath working on frozen pipes with a propane torch, or installing new ones with an instruction book lying open in the dirt in front of me. My mortgage was $600. I discovered anew how claustrophobic and narrowing it is to live with little money. (I'd known it in my childhood, too, although in a different way.) The amount of time and energy spent on small household and automotive tragedies. The frustration of not being able to go any-where more than ten miles away. The fact that even with long winter underwear it was cold. The brutality of the wind in February, humming through the thin spaces in the barn's oak siding.

I tried scallop fishing, but I wasn't strong enough and it was dangerous work. I kept warm many nights, and kept myself in beer, by shooting darts in a pub, as

I'd done at college. I spent the first winter like quite a few of the locals, simply waiting for summer.

"Don't sink," my lawyer had said on a brief visit to check up on me after the divorce. "Some guys just sink. Don't." He wasn't talking about boats.

Squirrels?

BECAUSE OF ITS PROXIMITY TO THE GULF Stream, Nantucket is usually 10 percent cooler than the mainland in the summer and 10 percent warmer in the winter. This means that usually you can get by with a couple of heavy sweaters (and the obligatory long underwear for those living in unheated barns) until Christmas. January, February, and March tend to be very windy, and somehow psychologically debilitating. Spring is a foreign concept on Nantucket. Sometimes it doesn't rain in April and May, and a lot of times it does. June is muddy.

Nevertheless there was something about this mild common hardship that drew people together, that helped to form the spirit of Nantucket, our "rock." In the seventies it was easy to meet people and make friends. A certain civility prevailed, presumably because there was no escape from each other. There were only so many places—be it The Hub, Cy's Green Coffee Pot, the Chicken Box—and you could be sure if you ran into somebody in one place you'd see them a couple of days later in another.

It was such a small town that sometimes odd, nice things would happen. Maggie, my girlfriend, lived on the westernmost edge of the island near Madaket Millie, I lived on Polpis Harbor halfway to 'Sconset. One week to the day after Maggie moved in with me her mail started to be delivered to my post office box. No instructions had been given, no forms filled out. It just happened. I imagine Sinclair Lewis would have thought it was terrible. We thought it was wonderful.

〰

THIRTY YEARS AGO the ferry ran from Woods Hole on the laconic Winter Schedule during the off-season, and on the expanded Summer Schedule during the season, which was a good deal shorter then than it is now. The ferry loomed large in those days, bringing copies of the *New York Times* to The Hub, the single store allowed to sell them, as well as bringing milk, meat and eggs, mail, lumber, and other essentials. The ferry was an institution, like the Atheneum, or the windmill, or the clock tower above the Unitarian church. It carried people, of course, but not many during the off-season. If you had to go to the main-

land to get a root canal or for some other essential business, stepping onto the ferry on your way back was like
stepping onto the island itself. You would probably
know more than half the people on board, and so the
almost three-hour ride would pass quickly if the sea
was calm. One felt halfway home.

Or, at least in the case of one island restaurateur,
perhaps more than that. With a weighted suitcase
strapped to each wrist, he stepped over the rail behind
a storage area and launched himself into Nantucket
Sound, never to be seen again. We all knew the poor
fellow, and no one was surprised, somehow.

⚒

IT ISN'T EASY to get across how fragile, how vul-
nerable the island really is. The words have been re-
peated so many times about so many places as to
become meaningless. Nantucket's highly exposed acres
contain about a third of the heath lands, or moors, in
America. Nantucket is not typically American, concerned with its large treasures like the Grand Canyon,
the redwoods, the Mississippi, or the deserts and
mountains. Nantucket is in the realm of the small.
The small but valuable endangered species such as the
piping plover, the Muskeget vole, the osprey. Dozens
of species of plants, mosses, berries, and grasses exist
nowhere else. The almost unbelievable complexity of

a hundred-square-yard salt marsh can be destroyed by one house too many, one failed septic system. Nantucket has a greater variety of vegetation than any other place similar in size in America.

Excluding marine species, and further excluding birds, animal life is less varied. Deer have become a pest as in so many other Eastern built-up areas where they must compete for space and rub shoulders with humans. (My wife cannot leave potted flowers on the deck at night. They'll be gone in the morning. Once a deer chased her into the shed.) Pheasant, rabbit, and feral cats survive in the scrub; turtles lumber from pond to pond.

But until fairly recently there were no squirrels. When we first came as college kids there were none, and no one could remember when there ever had been. The oral history tells of a truckload of lumber coming across from Woods Hole on the ferry with a family of stowaway squirrels sometime in the sixties. By the seventies people would occasionally call Wes Tiffany at the University of Massachusetts Field Station to report a sighting. By the eighties squirrels were all over the island, fighting for every tree, every sheltered area in the winter, every hollow log. They too had become pests.

When, much later, I started teaching on the mainland at various universities, The Barn was usually closed up for the winters and became, in its partially

sheltered location, attractive to mice, owls, and most
particularly to squirrels, who chewed through the
outside soffits under the eaves, created a large colony
and nursery comfortably insulated by chewed-up
quilts stolen from the inside of the house and stuffed,
piece by piece into the long, dark, and snug expanse
of the soffits area. When my middle son Will and our
friend Phil were watching a rental movie one October
evening, they became aware of a small group of squirrels watching along with them from one of the beams.
Although the philosophy of The Barn with regard to
other life forms had been pretty much live and let
live—we called it "organic living"—Will and Phil decided things had gone too far. The next day, using
borrowed thirty-foot aluminum ladders, they pried
open the long boards under the eaves and held on for
dear life as hundreds of terrified squirrels flew off in
every direction.

"The word is overused," Will told me on the telephone, "but it was *awesome.*"

This tribal catastrophe no doubt struck deeply into
the collective squirrel mythos, since, once the soffits
were rebuilt and the few holes covered with copper
sheathing, the rodents never returned. The Barn itself
must have taken on some powerful squirrel juju for it
to still be off limits after all these years, generation
after generation.

For many more years the open moors and bramble

teemed with dog ticks. Every dog owner's nightly ritual was to sit down with pooch and pull out blood-sucking insects by hand, and deposit them in a jar of kerosene or the like. A disagreeable nuisance, but then, with a degree of speed perhaps only possible on a small island, the dog ticks almost disappeared. I haven't seen one in the last ten years. (And my dog runs free, swims in the harbor, plays in the woods and the salt marsh.) An ecological mystery, followed by the less mysterious and no less sudden ubiquity of the tiny deer tick. A serious matter. Minuscule insects no bigger than the period at the end of this sentence, catching the occasional ride with a mouse or a deer, latching on to tall grass, reeds, wildflowers, waiting it seems, for a human to come along. Finding skin soft enough and thin enough to penetrate and begin the exchange, the tick takes blood while leaving behind the spirochete for Lyme disease or the germ for babeseosis. This sets the stage for potentially danger-ous afflictions, which most people shake off, but others endure for years, worrying about the rare com-plications involving damage to the heart and the ner-vous system. In the summer, at a lawn party, it is not unusual to see a young woman with a small I.V. drip attached somewhere on her person, the thin plastic tube running down her bare arm to the firmly taped needle on the inside of her wrist. Continuous, long-term antibiotic therapy that doesn't interfere with mobility. A perverse kind of jewelry. An island status symbol.

If there were any Indians left, and were there a shaman among them, he might speak of the land resisting interference from humans. The need to dominate nature is deep inside us all. Lawns, for instance, are a statement of ownership, dominion, and what used to be called husbandry. On the mainland lawns seem innocuous enough, but as more and more of them are created on Nantucket problems have arisen. Chemicals seeping into the ground water, nitrogen from fertilizer impacting the marshes, ponds, and inlets. (When I built the barn in '69 we went down ten feet for water. Modernizing the plumbing in 1998 we thought it prudent to go down ninety feet, where the water is presumably purer.) People are advised to wear masks when they mow, because the lawn grass attracts rabbits whose dung lies uncovered, becomes powdered and airborne from the force of the mower blades, and sometimes has the power to sicken unto death. In terms of their ecological impact, no one knows how many lawns the island can sustain, even as more are cultivated. Fifty years ago it seemed people took pleasure in the unique, delicate wilderness of the island. Now it seems people are coming for different reasons, and may be made slightly uneasy by what they misperceive as bleakness. So they "improve" their plot of land.

The White Elephant Gig

IT WAS MY SECOND WINTER ON NANTUCKET when I first learned my social security number by heart. The unemployment office was a fairly large room on the second floor of the American Legion Hall at the edge of town. People sat on benches, in an arrangement reminiscent of church, facing a large desk behind which sat Wendy, an aging waitress familiar to all of us, who'd been lucky enough to snag a state job in the off-season. She would pull out a file, call the number, and if it was yours, you went up to go through the formalities and get your check. Although she knew just about everybody in the room on a first-name basis, she was all business, never so much as cracking a smile or giving any sign of recognition. It seemed a bit overdone to me, since on Nantucket there was certainly no shame attached to being on unemployment or using food stamps. Half the working people of the island were on unemployment. I was eligible because I'd played the piano at a fancy hotel six nights a week for three and a half months during the previous summer.

It was (and still is) called the White Elephant and was owned by Sherburne, which was mostly owned by Mr. Beineke. Beineke had a manservant, a middle-aged Italian I will call Flavianno, who had been Mr. Beineke's favorite towel boy at the New York Athletic Club, and whom he had hired away from that famous and exclusive institution to serve the Beineke household in various capacities.

One of Flavianno's responsibilities was to keep an eye on the restaurant, the bar, and the piano lounge. He did not run these parts of the hotel, but simply dropped in every now and then, making his rounds and trying to look important. He made it clear he had no use for me, or for the jazz I played, or for the mostly young and informal crowd I drew. He once made a waiter throw out a gay couple because they were in violation of the dress code, which called for jackets. From that night on I kept two or three jackets stashed behind the bandstand to lend to people who might need them. He was furious of course, and for the rest of the summer harassed me, cursed me to my face, and presumably tried to get me fired. But I was breaking records for bar sales, and pulling in people for the restaurant. Everybody was making money and there would have been protests from the staff. He had to be content with trying to push me to the point where I would lose my temper and do something rash, but I kept my cool.

It was an uncomfortable situation, to be sure, but not without a momentary silver lining.

I should explain that I had a remote connection to the Kennedy family. My older sister's husband had run Jack's presidential campaign in Madison, Wisconsin, so I had tagged along to the inaugural. When Bobby eventually ran, Norman Mailer and I were to read at a fund-raiser at Town Hall in New York. Bobby was assassinated two days before the event, which of course did not take place. The Kennedy organization was nothing if not efficient, so years later, when Senator Ted came over to Nantucket for a small cocktail party/fund-raiser at Beineke's house, the organization somehow knew I was on the island and sent me an invitation. The party conflicted with my schedule in the piano lounge (I played two shifts, one before dinner and one after) but I didn't hesitate, and showed up at Beineke's right on time. He introduced himself—we had never met, nor was he aware of my employment at the hotel. We made small talk as other people began arriving. When he moved away, Senator Kennedy came in from the dining room and caught my eye. We stood together talking for several moments when someone offered us a tray of hors d'oeuvres. "These little toasted things are good," Teddy said to me. "Try one."

Flavianno stood holding the tray.

"I will," I said, looking my nemesis straight in the eye, reaching out slowly, my hand hovering over the plate to draw out the moment. Not my finest hour, perhaps, but one which I nevertheless enjoyed. Nantucket was a very small place back then, and such things could happen. Flavianno never bothered me again.

Golf Games

*I*CAME TO GOLF FAIRLY LATE IN LIFE, WHEN two of my pals more or less forced me to go over to Skinner's and give it a try. Skinner's—I can't remember its official name, but Skinner Coffin ran the place—was an ancient nine-hole course open to all at a dollar a hole. Nothing fancy, but well maintained. Phil and Tom gave me a few pointers, showed me how to hold the club, told me to keep my head down during the swing, and finally teed me up. I addressed the ball with a two-iron, swung smoothly, and got off a clean, straight shot that soared out 110 yards to land at the edge of the green, where it proceeded to run up halfway to the pin.

"Hey! This is fun!" I said. "I see what you guys mean."

Tom gave me a slightly puzzled look. Phil just laughed. It would be two years and hundreds of missed, bungled, dribbling, slicing, hooking shots later before I managed to drive to that particular green again. I turned out to be a poor golfer, shooting in the high nineties most days while Phil and Tom cruised along in the low eighties. I kept on, though, unable to forget the almost orgasmic thrill of that first shot.

We were three guys from very different backgrounds who enjoyed one another's company. (A few winters on the island and you found out who you liked pretty rapidly.) Tom, from the South, was a builder, soon to invent a one-handed pepper mill (The Peppergun!) and make his fortune. Phil came from Indiana and worked as a master carpenter as well as sommelier during the season. I was a writer from New York. The game of golf brought us even closer together, and that was definitely one of its pleasures.

The rituals were reassuring. Everybody had to show up, first of all, each of us by that act recommitting ourselves to a certain tacit camaraderie. Gathering at the first tee, fussing with our bags and carts, there was a pleasant sense of anticipation. We knew exactly what we would be doing for the next hour and a half, and we knew exactly the parameters of our activity—drive, approach, putt, move to the next hole, and do it again. A comfortable rhythm at a comfortable pace. There was no sense of competition—even between Tom and Phil, who played at more or less the same level of skill—rather the sense that each individual was playing against himself, against the maddening vagaries of golf itself, so deceptively simple on the surface, so infinitely complex underneath. For us there were no external variables except, occasionally, the wind. The challenge was almost entirely unchanging and static—the pesky fourth hole always the same every time you approached. The variables were within—inside our individual bodies and minds. Which is why the game can drive people nuts. Which is why it's probably not such a good idea to play the game alone for any length of time.

We knew the story of Chester Wilmont, after all, the local lawyer, unmarried, upstanding citizen, on the town board, etc., who played Skinner's every day, always alone, sometimes mumbling abstractedly or making gestures in the air. It was Skinner himself, lounging on the porch of the clubhouse, who watched him five-putt the fourth hole and sat transfixed while Chester, a big man, removed one by one the clubs he had inherited from his father, breaking them over his knee, taking off his shoes, and leaving everything—bag, busted irons, shoes, balls, tees, scorecard, pencils—right there on the grass. He walked to his car without looking back and was never seen on a Nantucket golf course again.

"He got too deep in the tunnel," Phil explained.

"What tunnel?" I asked.

"The tunnel of self," Tom said.

"I bet he birdied the first three holes."

They nodded together and shook their heads at the folly of mankind.

My first season was to spend time in the tunnel myself—frustration, anger, the desire to rush or to do it over, to sink into strings of mulligans—but my friends always pulled me out with a word or two. They knew how lucky we were playing on such a beautiful course, high on the island with views of the sea, and never crowded. (It was this extraordinary natural beauty, no doubt, that led to the recent construction of an eighteen-hole course just a half mile away. An exclusive club whose memberships go at three hundred thousand dollars a pop. I kid you not.) I became familiar with an inherent tension in the game that first season—contemplation of the calm beauty of nature, the immutable physical reality of the course itself, the fairways, the greens, even the slowly changing colors of the rough, in other words the *outside,* against the need to maintain an emotional calmness on the *inside,* to maintain a sense of balance between yourself and the world as you walked through the game and its tests.

So we took golf fairly seriously those first couple of years—nothing obsessive, but we treated the experience with respect. We went out to the other end of the island and tried the links at Miacomet, which was in those days a mildly funky workingman's course, with beer, hot dogs, and potato chips. We were not snobs, but when a couple of guys from the lumber yard teed off in front of us with some special gizmo that allowed them to hit the ball at waist level with a baseball bat, we went back to the simplicity at Skinner's. We got ourselves invited to the old Sankaty Head Golf Club and played what must be one of the most gorgeous eighteen-hole courses in the Northeast. It seemed odd to ride the golf carts, however, as if a certain purity was lost.

It may be that if you learn the game late in life, the particular course you learn on has a kind of lock on you you'll never escape. For me, the only course that counts is Skinner's. Only on those nine holes can I measure my progress (if indeed there is any) or feel any real sense of accomplishment. Maybe I got too serious, but for one reason or another by the third year the element of laughter—which had always been there to some extent—began to blossom in our threesome. Phil was a brilliant mimic, with dozens of accents and characters in his repertoire, and was capable of switching personae during the course of the game. I believe that was how it started. Not jokes, but entirely free improvisation, spontaneous role-playing, and other nonsense in a sort of Marx Brothers–Monty Python hybrid. We got really silly, in a way that would probably not have been possible in any other setting. In terms of my golf scores, I had more or less reached my individual plateau, going up or down only a few points from one game to the next. And so, with a kind of mild and delicious hysteria, we began to deconstruct the game of golf, or rather to deconstruct our behavior while playing it.

Oh, there's really no way to adequately describe it, or to directly describe it, but the fact is I would sometimes simply fall to the grass helpless with laughter at some riff of Phil's as a Pakistani intellectual, or at our collective serial description of a Stalinist golf course, or some other foolishness. I remember once as Tom and I sat on the bench at the seventh—a "smoking hole" by tradition, Phil with his Old Golds, Tom with Marlboros, and myself with Merits (we have all since stopped)—while Phil teed up, bent over to pluck an offending blade of grass, and fiddled around as usual. Finally, he was ready. Tom and I maintained the silence and stillness appropriate to this charged moment. Phil took his backswing as usual, but then instead of keeping his head down he raised it and looked directly into my eyes. He twisted his face into a mask, into some demented gargoyle, and never broke eye contact with me as he swung, catching the ball perfectly for a 150-yard drive. Then, he winked.

Or the day when we agreed that I simply swung too fast, that I should work on smoothing things out. So I tried singing, just a phrase of something familiar as I commenced my backswing—"Some day my PRINCE will come"—timing it all so I'd hit the ball at the word *prince*. The boys thought this was a swell idea, and we made a rule that for the rest of the week everybody would have to do it on the fourth and fifth holes.

"People, people who need PEOPLE . . ." or "I'll be down to get you in a TAXI, honey," or "I get no KICK from champagne."

Eventually we moved on to a variation in which the word "lunch" had to be substituted wherever the lyric said "love."

"I can't give you anything but LUNCH, baby." Or "Once I had a secret LUNCH."

Oh my goodness, we laughed. And it felt wonderful.

And so I was released. We all knew I was never going to be good enough to play at the high levels that can keep the game fascinating for a lifetime. I didn't have to break my clubs over my knee like poor old Chester. I went out laughing.

I think I can remember the precise afternoon when I sensed that the game of golf was perhaps not going to be the game for me. The sixth at Skinner's is a long par five, and the first part is a gentle hill, but I could never make it even as far as the top. After one such attempt I sighed and said, "It sure would be nice to get over the damn thing."

We started forward, pulling our carts behind us.

"Well," Phil said gently, "if it hasn't happened by now, the chances are it never will."

All too true. I haven't hit a golf ball for at least nineteen years.

The Roadhouse

"Down for the summer?"

I winced when Hank Kahlenback, Nantucket old boy and manager of the Pacific Bank, asked me the question with a wry smile. I had taken a job teaching in America (as some old-timers called the mainland) and was no longer a year-rounder. I had lost much of that status. Now I was "summer people." Well, not quite, because I had left my mark.

In the '70s I got together with two island pals, one of whom, thank God, had some money, and went into business. We leased an old, failed bar way out of town, a simple place that years ago had served pilots and crew from the airport and the Navy base (since closed) after hours. We called it the Roadhouse, and the idea was that the club was to be ours, the year-rounders, and to hell with the summer people. The dynamic resembled the old Mickey Rooney–Judy Garland idea, "Hey,

kids, let's put on a show!" We threw ourselves into it
with tremendous enthusiasm, and without a trace of
cynicism. (As it turned out, our lack of cynicism was
not entirely a good thing.) It was a big job and many
friends volunteered their help. Carpenters remodeled
the old bar and added an extension into the music
room; the incredibly filthy kitchen out back was
cleaned and rebuilt; tables, chairs, linens, glasses, and
bar equipment were borrowed, leased, or bought.
Partner A saw to the acquisition of pertinent licenses,
permissions, etc., as well as overseeing the remodeling
and fronting significant amounts of cash. Partner B
interviewed people for staff, made arrangements with
wholesalers for the booze and the food, acted as manager of everything during (and after) the chaos, and
Partner C (that's me) put together a hard-swinging
blues, bebop quintet and ran rehearsals even as the
club was being built around us.

The band included a black tenor sax player from
Boston, a Jewish intellectual from New York on alto
and flute, a series of drummers over time, a local bass
player who died from cocaine and was replaced by a
kid from the Cape, and myself on piano. A classic jazz
quintet, with acoustic instruments and no gimmicks.
We worked hard at rehearsal, putting together jazz
standards, our own tunes, good vamps to play "free"
improvisations, and developing a distinctive, balanced
sound. It was a lot of fun. A high-energy band, every-

one agreed. The club looked classy when we opened, like a real nightclub/roadhouse from a Bogart movie. It was an instant hit.

In fact it became an institution of sorts (albeit short-lived) for islanders and eventually for a rather select group of summer people. Recently Partner B wrote a note for a vanity CD of the band, ". . . musicians of blossoming eminence crystallized a unique time and place, a few years in a roadside joint that will never repeat. Our lives are dated by before the Roadhouse, the Roadhouse, and since the Roadhouse. [There are] countless unrecorded stories we all have to tell."

Too many to tell here, certainly, but I'll share a few. Typically the place did not fill until about 10 P.M. for several reasons: There was no air-conditioning, a lot of the audience didn't get off work till then, it was isolated and out of town so you had to drive or get a ride (no public transportation then), and perhaps its history as an "after hours" place was part of it. The cops gave us maybe half an hour longer than the bars in town, but still we had to make the day's money in three and a half hours. A cover charge or a minimum was, we all agreed, impossible, given the spirit of the place. We could not charge more for drinks than other places for the same reason. It seemed to me that all we could do was encourage our customers to drink "top shelf" where our profit margin was slightly higher.

Consequently I placed an ice bucket with a bottle of champagne in full view beside me at the piano. After every tune I'd pour myself a glass. The theory was, as I explained to my partners, that some customers would think if the piano player can drink champagne instead of beer then why the hell can't I?

It might not have worked in an ordinary club, but the Roadhouse had a special atmosphere, a celebratory mood because it was "our" place, where the champagne was indeed champagne, but also a kind of in joke among working people, a sort of parody of the Toffs drinking Veuve Cliquot at the Chanticleer or the Opera House. (Those years were perhaps the last years when the young year-rounders had a sense of themselves as an entity, a discrete group constituting a half-hidden subculture within the population.) Of course it didn't hurt that a lot of people felt fairly loose and impulsive by the time they got out to the club, where they knew they would end the evening. The wine wholesalers told us that in our second and third years of operation we sold more champagne than any other bar/restaurant on the island.

Boy, was it a "happening" place, and boy did we have fun! The audience was completely with us, the same couple of hundred people coming night after night, week after week. I remember looking up after a particularly hot tune to see people standing on chairs against the walls, smiling, shouting, urging us on, every table filled with truly happy people. The consensus among the musicians in the band, and the growing number of players coming over from Boston to hear us (and sometimes sit in), was that it was the ultimate "dream gig."

As it turned out we were the victims of our own success, our lack of business experience, and our naive belief in the basic honesty of people. The Roadhouse certainly looked like it was doing well. So many customers wanted to get in the fire marshal made us hire a door person, a nice-guy bouncer, so as not to exceed the legal limit of 225 persons. On any given night there would be fifty or more people out in the parking lot or gathered around the windows, listening, hoping to get in. Customers stood three deep at the bars in both rooms and we were forced to hire bartenders we didn't know very well, waitresses we didn't know very well, and things just got too big and too fast.

It took us a long time to realize how much money was slipping away each night. We had all agreed to split the "skim" (the 10 percent off the top the state more or less expected would be taken) and give the rest to that partner who'd put up most of the money in the first place (after payroll, of course). The partner was getting practically nothing, but he was having so much fun, along with the rest of us, that he was loath to blow the whistle. The skim was enough to get by on, and we let things slide.

Roadhouse band.

Someone, or some people, were stealing, and we did not know how to stop it. We hadn't a clue. We were working very hard for what turned out to be an enterprise we agreed to remember as some kind of weird cooperative, in what was the longest, best party anyone could ever hope to attend. There was sadness all around when we finally threw in the towel.

When I remember the Roadhouse it isn't just the club that comes to mind. Yes, lots of stories, weddings, friendships, and so forth, but I'll just tell my favorite. Let's call him Nick. He came to Nantucket as a young man, working as a roustabout for the moderately cheesy traveling carnival that came every year. He liked the island and decided to stay. Partner B hired him to do the kitchen—to draw up a simple menu and do the cooking. Simple was definitely the concept, since even back then the Nantucket restaurant scene was as competitive and cutthroat as New York's. Just burgers and the like—a gastronomic low profile. We were not trying to make a statement with the food, but Nick wasn't bothered by our lack of courage. He needed to be left alone in his *mise* with his pots and pans and his ancient stove. We were very busy and forgot all about him until people started talking about the chili. "Where'd you get this guy? That's the best chili I've ever had in my life." Nick turned out to be a natural. He was fast, smart, incapable of panic, with good hands—all the basics—but also the owner of a sensitive palate, an innate love of food and the pleasures of food, and an almost religious obsession with the importance of presentation. He was very, very careful in his work.

Clever, too. The menu looked simple. Burgers, fries, chili, salad, the accoutrements, the little side dishes of thin french-fried onions, the cornichons, crab cakes, and the like. Customers discovered his food gradually, as he slipped in a changing series of goodies, special surprises every now and then, making the diner feel special.

The restaurant people of the island—the chefs, sous-chefs, dishwashers, waiters, maître d's, and bartenders—were an important part of our clientele. When the Roadhouse closed, Nick had no problem getting a job and beginning serious study of what he now knew would be his life's work. Over the years he rose through the ranks in several fine restaurants and became the sous-chef at the Club Car, where the marvelously talented Michael Shannon taught him everything he needed to know. And then some.

Nick had lived sensibly on Nantucket, staying away from the expensive fads of recreational drugs or the heavy drinking so often to be found on islands. He was a steady, easygoing guy who planned, waited patiently for years, and finally bought a small restaurant in which he proceeded to make five- and six-course dinners good enough to bring tears to one's eyes.

The restaurant is still there, flourishing despite the intensity of the competition, because Nick knew exactly the niche he wanted and precisely how to control it. Nothing like this could happen now, of course. For a man to arrive with nothing but character, talent, patience, and a work ethic—for such a man to arrive, grow, get his restaurant, and build a comfortable home for himself and his wife is no longer possible. Today he'd have to step out of the airplane with two or three million dollars, a lot of powerful contacts, and a phenomenal amount of luck. Probably even Nick couldn't do it today.

It isn't that kind of place anymore.

〰

PLEASE TAKE A look at a map of Nantucket. Run your finger from Madaket down the coast to the south shore, and then along the bottom of the island and up to 'Sconset. As Nancy Chase explains in *We Are Nantucket:*

> *The south shore . . . all the way from Madaket to 'Sconset . . . that's the south shore. Very few houses were built there because . . . the next time you went there, it wasn't there. Somebody stole it! Took the wood and stuff because of scarcity of wood on the Island. Nobody was there. Nobody to see you take it.*

It is unclear exactly what time period Nancy Chase is referring to. She was born on the island in 1931, so she could be talking about just about any time up to, say, the fifties. Nowadays there are hundreds of houses along the same stretch. And thousands of squirrels of course.

BUMPER STICKERS are displayed by year-rounders on the back of their pick-ups or old cars as a kind of self-affirmation, as well as a way to communicate with each other while differentiating themselves from the summer people.

IT'S NICER ON NANTUCKET

was followed many years later by:

IT USED TO BE NICER ON NANTUCKET

A favorite of fishermen, scallopers, and pilots:

FOG HAPPENS

In protest against a development plan that was eventually shot down by the town:

NO MOOR HOUSES

In protest of another proposed mid-island development which would have included a large new supermarket:

BAG THE MARKET

The plan failed.

Third World Softball

L AST SUMMER A FRIEND CAME BY FOR ICED tea on the deck, a woman my wife and I think of as one of our old crowd. "We had the best," she said. "The seventies were the best." Each generation seems to remember a time when things were best. For Robert Mooney it is perhaps the forties, when people sang songs on Main Street and everybody went home at ten, when there were no tourists or day-trippers, just some townspeople and the summer people. Some remember the sixties and a bar at the foot of Main Street called the Bosun's Locker, a hangout that spilled outside to the cobblestones where the marijuana smoke drifted freely and people laughed and danced.

A special memory of my own involves the evolution of what came to be known as Third World Softball. Like any small town, Nantucket had a league of sorts—the oil company, Yates welders, First National,

Don Allen Ford, and others, all fielded teams and played on the high school diamond. A fairly insular bunch of big strong guys who took the game seriously. No room, really, for unaffiliated people.

How old were my boys then? Eight and ten, perhaps? (Grown now with boys of their own.) My few friends, a carpenter/inventor, a sommelier, an actor, the camera shop owner with the braid down his back, were all unaffiliated. Waiters, waitresses, bartenders, friends of my wife's—these were the people we raised a glass with at the Ship's Inn or Cy's Green Coffee Pot. It started one Sunday afternoon when a few of us took the boys out to the deserted, mildly overgrown softball field next to the water company shack in 'Sconset. We hit a few soft ground balls, shagged flies, played catch with the boys, and sat on the old benches chewing the fat.

Over time enough people heard about it, or saw it from the road and stopped to join in, that we realized we could make up sides, which changed every week except for the captains, myself and the camera shop guy, whose name was Gene. We were also the pitchers. Slow pitches, so that my kids could play with a minimum of fear.

Rules emerged through a semi-democratic process. For some reason it was particularly satisfying as the rules were realized.

Starting time, 2 P.M. every Sunday

*Women and children welcomed and guaranteed a
spot (even if right field)*

No aluminum bats

No beer

No radios

High standards of sportsmanship

Eventually, it became a tradition, each year of play
marked by its own T-shirt.

Nothing was ever formalized beyond these rules.
No records were kept. Whoever showed up showed
up ("Where's Freddie?" Pause. "Hung over."), and
there were always more than enough players. As time
went on, and my sons got through their growth and
began to be picked first, there were even spectators on
the benches. It was a completely spontaneous happening, and it lasted thirteen years. Thirteen years! But
we'd never registered anywhere, or even thought of
reserving the field, which we'd taken for granted for
so long—and when the island grew and the "First
World" league grew also, they took the field away
from us. Nantucket was changing, we all knew, but the
loss of Third World Softball was particularly painful.

Third World Softball.

A very, very rich man who lived on the other side of the island in a sprawling compound of many houses, an artificial lake, a small golf course, and an officially correct, perfectly groomed softball field complete with dugouts, bleachers, etc., built on a whim, heard about our eviction and offered his own "field of dreams." And it *was* like something out of a dream. A beautiful, virgin field. We started playing again with enthusiasm, which mysteriously and unsettlingly began to wane. Each Sunday a few more people couldn't make it. The vibe changed. It became something of a duty. No one bothered us, or watched us, and yet it lost its spirit. It became artificial, somehow, which perhaps had something to do with the obscene amount of money poured into the setting. The poshness, the very perfection of the field overwhelmed the games we played on it. More people dropped. When Gene was given a box of legal releases, one to be signed by each player before each game, Third World Softball lost its soul entirely and stopped. It was over. Generosity had killed it and after thirteen years it was gone forever.

SOME YEARS AGO an eccentric British mathematician, whose name I have forgotten, played around with Einstein's equations and came up with a model of the universe in which time is accelerating, infinitely. In other words, the reason it seems time is going faster as we get older is because it *is* going faster. (Einstein was polite, but unimpressed.) So one's perception would be marked by when one got on the train, so to speak. Where you got on is normal, and then things speed up.

Something like that goes on in people's thoughts and feelings about Nantucket. What was normal for Mooney's people was changed by the time my college friends and I showed up in the late fifties. Most of the people who have arrived on the island, or have discovered the island in, say, the past ten years, are convinced that it is something close to perfect. The physical beauty of the moors, the deep beaches, the salt marshes, the splendid harbor, the light, the salt air, the freshness are unique and precious. It is only later that the question of critical mass might come up. How much humanity can the island hold? Is it possible that Nantucket could become a sort of aircraft carrier of expensive homes? A kind of platform out at sea? How real is the danger? Can anything be done? These are truly difficult questions, and I certainly can't answer them.

How About Manners?

THE MARKETPLACE IS ALWAYS OF SPECIAL interest to anthropologists, archaeologists, historians, and the like. I suppose the idea is that what goes on in the markets reveals the society itself to some extent. That is certainly true for the "Gray Lady of the Sea."

The Cumberland Farm store on the east side of town is a convenience store now—cigarettes, Twinkies, canned soup, Wonder bread, and so on—but it started out a long time ago as a sort of cooperative, organized by some local moms who were fed up with the high price of milk at the supermarket and decided to do something about it. It was true then, and it is true now, that almost everything is marked up in Nantucket. Gasoline, for instance, is quite a lot higher than on the Cape. There is more competition now—more markets (lots of boutique markets, specialty meat markets, a couple of farmer's markets, one of them huge), but prices are still high—no longer due to what you might call captive customers (not so long ago there was only that one place to get the Sunday *New York Times,* The Hub, smack in the middle of downtown at the corner of Main and Federal), but because of the generally "up" market of people who don't have to worry what a quart of milk might cost. Of course, it is a seasonal economy, and retailers have to survive in February as well as August.

The general priciness perhaps reaches its extremes at the 'Sconset Market, the only grocery store in the village at the eastern end of the island, where the prices of ordinary items like a bag of Oreos or a box of cereal are so astronomical it takes one's breath away. (They do bake some very fine baguettes, in their defense.) But no one does major shopping there. For that one goes to the supermarket—either the rather modestly sized Grand Union built as part of the downtown wharf development project, or most important the huge Stop and Shop at the edge of town. It was once a Finast, and before that something else, but it has always been the dominant market, and increasingly so as the island has grown to the point where there are more people living out of town (in season, at least) than in town. The Stop and Shop is it, and they must be commended for an honest effort to keep their prices reasonable, not too much more than in their stores on the mainland.

My ex-wife, who lives out west, was struck by the change in atmosphere at the market when she visited the island a couple of summers ago. She remembered a kind of community spirit—high school kids or working college kids at the checkouts, people chatting with friends in the aisles, a certain social cohesiveness—that wasn't there anymore. From the insanely crowded parking lot, with everyone honking horns, jostling for spaces, bumping bumpers, to the jam-packed aisles of people racing inside, eager to get back to the beach or the barbecue, it has a frantic, almost desperate feel in the high season. One rarely recognizes anyone now—to come upon a friend or acquaintance at the deli section is rare indeed, and invariably creates a certain nostalgia for the old days. The checkout staff, the baggers, and the like are mostly Jamaicans now, speaking a bewildering patois, unconnected, like migrant workers (which they are), from the culture around them. It is a pressured atmosphere, and not comfortable or enjoyable. It's a pain in the ass, in fact, for a lot of us.

Four or five years ago my wife was witness to a scene in the supermarket that may be emblematic of the transformation of Nantucket from a small town into something else altogether. A prominent family on the island whom I will call the Smiths—summer people for generations—were involved in various local businesses at a high level. Bob Smith is a big, handsome guy with a thousand-watt smile, a lot of charm, and a lot of smarts. His image on the island was carefully cultivated—an honest, thoughtful, family man with good values and a heightened sense of community. And all of this was, and no doubt still is, true. Which makes what my wife saw all the more astonishing.

The Stop and Shop, on a Friday afternoon, was jam-packed with shoppers stocking up for the weekend, anticipating guests, jostling up and down the aisles in a mild frenzy. My wife was waiting in line at one of the checkout lanes. She sees Bob moving forward with a cart filled to the brim, top to bottom, and inserting himself into the express lane. The girl at the cash register protests. "This is twelve items only," she says. "This is the express lane."

Smiling his warm, knock-'em-dead smile, Bob reaches up and slides the little placard which says "Express Lane" from its holder and puts it facedown next to the register. "Not anymore, it isn't," he declares, and begins to unload his stuff. Flummoxed, the girl waits a moment, looks around, and then goes ahead and starts the long process of ringing things up. There is some grumbling from the line behind Bob, but no one has the nerve to protest. Bob no longer cares what people think. His assumption is that he'll never see any of the other shoppers again.

I am reminded of a scene in John Cheever's last book, *Oh What a Paradise It Seems*. (Cheever was a great fan of the island in its simpler days, but stopped coming when his favorite hotel—an old, rundown place with remarkable views—was demolished to be replaced by a stratospherically expensive luxury establishment.) Although the setting is not Nantucket, the scene is prophetic.

Maybelle was the name of the checkout clerk and she wore a large pin that said so. "Maybelle," said Betsy, "would you kindly explain to this lady that this lane is the express lane for shoppers with nine items only." "If she can't read I'm not going to teach her," said Maybelle. The twelve or so members in the line behind Betsy showed their approval. "It's about time somebody said something" . . . "You tell 'em, lady, you tell 'em," said an old man with a frozen dinner. "I just can't stand to see someone take advantage of other people's kindness. It's like fascism. It isn't that she's breaking the law. It's just that most of us are too nice to do anything about it. Why do you suppose they put up a sign that says nine items? It's to make the store more efficient for everyone. You're just like a shoplifter, only you're not stealing groceries, you're stealing time, you're not stealing from the management, you're stealing from us."

Cheever continues the story until civil behavior breaks down and a minor riot ensues. It's a comic scene with an edge, but an important moment in the text. (Neither my wife nor myself have ever felt quite the same toward old Bob, who has gone on to be a tremendous success in the world of finance.)

Let's See to the Land

THERE ARE TWO FARMS ON NANTUCKET. THE first, Moors End Farm, off Polpis Road, is a small family affair selling a few vegetables, lots of flowers and plants, and, in August, a large crop of the sweetest, whitest, most tender corn imaginable. No sprays or pesticides, and no opening the ears looking for worms. You buy a dozen or so ears and go your merry way. (It is exceedingly rare to find a less than perfect ear.) Although the farm does good business, and is in fact beloved by many islanders, it was almost lost due to economic pressures. The value of an acre of land—any acre—has gotten so high, and the taxes too, that farming is impractical, or would have been if the town, relevant organizations, and interested islanders hadn't managed to pass special legislation and make financial arrangements to ensure its survival.

The other farm—Bartlett's—also a family affair

but much larger, a very big business indeed, growing many crops, selling sandwiches, gourmet salads, frozen foods, fancy breads, pastries, cheeses, fruit, and so on, was also saved by special arrangements, despite its fancy airs, greenhouses, and expensive equipment. There was a broad consensus on island that the farms, and their open spaces, must be preserved.

There have been quite a few people, for quite some time, highly concerned about development on Nantucket. Robert Mooney's book *Nantucket Only Yesterday* teaches the history of the struggle between those attempting to control growth and those resisting any infringement of their freedom to do as they like with their land. (Many working and middle-class families on the island really have nothing else except their land—it is their equity.) The back-and-forth tug of war between different parties, organizations, and local government and interest groups, is a long-standing affair, going back many decades.

There is the Land Council, and I quote from their mission statement: "We negotiate with private owners to voluntarily restrict use of their land and preserve conservation values. These permanent easement agreements—conservation restrictions in Massachusetts—provide public benefits to the community and handsome tax advantages to landowners . . ." In other words, they have done the legal work so that anyone who wants to enter into such an arrangement can do so without hassle or out-of-pocket expenses. They also raise funds, clear title to hundreds of acres of vacant land, and work to protect water resources, among other things. (Nantucket has been designated a sole source aquifer by the U.S. Environmental Protection Agency.)

The Nantucket Land Bank is based on the proposition that it takes money to defend against money. In 1983 the Land Bank (Chapter 669) was created in law, ". . . a land conservation program created to acquire, hold, and manage important open space resources and endangered landscapes . . ." The money used to buy land on the open market is acquired by a 2 percent real estate transfer fee on almost every house or parcel of land that gets sold. A powerful idea indeed, put forward by the Nantucket Planning Commission, adopted by the voters of Nantucket and established by a special act of the state legislature. . . . Approximately 40 percent of Nantucket is protected by private conservation groups, the Town of Nantucket, and the Land Bank. Big money—almost a hundred million dollars—has worked to protect land. The Land Bank often operates in tandem with the Nantucket Conservation Foundation, and there is little doubt that they have saved entire parts of the island.

My house is just 1.3 miles from Altar Rock, the highest point on the island. For years my family has driven, jogged, or walked inland to visit the spot from which you can see hundreds and hundreds of acres of open moors, completely wild except for the ancient dirt tracks like the Barnard Valley Road, or old short cuts to the South Shore. It is a breathtaking panorama—one can see the harbor in the distance, Sankaty lighthouse, the low tree lines of distant hidden forests of scrub oak. Without protection, houses, developments, mini-villages, and the like would be scattered all the way across the interior. Action was taken in the nick of time. Public action, not dependent on philanthropy. This particular part of the island was saved—a part of the 40 percent. The conservation movement has grown stronger over time, although there is still much to be done.

Ironically, a proposal put forward by Senator Edward Kennedy in 1972—The Nantucket Sound and Islands Trust Bill—would have accomplished everything on the conservationists' agenda, and then some, making great tracts of land on both Nantucket and Martha's Vineyard "forever wild" as well as strictly controlling new construction. In hindsight such an action was clearly the way to go and would have benefited everyone—islanders and summer people alike. But the residents of Nantucket voted against the bill, presumably out of fear of Federalism, loss of control of their destiny and their equity, and other boogeymen. Perhaps the bill would have died at the federal level no matter what the local vote, but at a special town meeting in 1976, Nantucket "lost forever the possibility of preserving its shoreline for the public benefit . . ." as Mr. Mooney put it. (He also makes the point that there have been some pretty strange votes on the island over time, like the resounding yes vote for a downsizing of the state legislature, which resulted in the loss of the Nantucket seat. A self-imposed partial disenfranchment, in other words.)

The Kennedy bill would have effectively prevented the expensive, complicated, and sometimes controversial growth of local government caused by a patchwork of zoning, planning boards, appeals procedures, building regulations, etc., involving more committees, more civil servants, more legal fees, and more paper. The history of the Historic District Commission is an example of the inappropriateness (or so it seems to me) of the kind of reflexive expansion of activity that sometimes weakens a good idea.

The original concept was to protect that beautiful part of town behind the Pacific National Bank that I described earlier. So far, so good. The impact of a modern structure, or a bad remodeling, would have had a horrendous effect on the area, destroying its integrity. But when the "Historic District" was expanded to include the whole island, a lot of people were unhappy, even to the point of flaunting the regulations. Who says I have to use cedar shingles as siding? Who says, since my house is hidden from public view, I can't put in a bay window, or paint my fence green, or build an extension? Who says my projected dream house cannot exceed a certain height even if I build it in the middle of a fifty-acre lot?

The expansion has given rise to the worst possible outcome—some people obey the law, and some people get away with ignoring it, since, from a practical point of view, it can't be well enforced. It may even be unconstitutional. One wonders sometimes if the powers that be on Nantucket don't regard the Constitution as just another bit of Federalism, or the Supreme Court as nothing more than a bunch of off-islanders who can't be expected to understand.

A long time ago there was a bumper sticker which said, simply:

NANTUCKET

A young woman of my acquaintance,
who would occasionally appear in town in
a full chador just for the fun of it
(she's a WASP), slapped on an addition every
time she found one:

ALAS NANTUCKET

The generally somber tone is not to be
taken too seriously. It is more nostalgia
than pessimism.

Degrees of Erosion

*I*SLANDERS SOMETIMES REFER TO NANTUCKET as "The Rock," calling up images of the Prudential (a piece of the rock, i.e., a buildable lot) as well as Alcatraz (for some the island is indeed a kind of prison). But the reality is that it's more like a heap of sand, constantly changing shape under the influence of wind and water. There are eighty-eight miles of shoreline, and more than half of it is subject to varying degrees of erosion. The lighthouse at Great Point, a historic structure if there ever was one, collapsed into the sea in 1984. (A replacement was built with federal funds, thanks to the efforts of Senator Kennedy.) Over four hundred feet of land separating the lighthouse and the ocean had simply disappeared.

The whole length of the South Shore faces the open ocean—the nearest land to the east being Portugal—and suffers dramatic and unpredictable erosion from winter storms. Through the years people have built too close to the surf, as if unaware of what has happened in the past, and many houses have been lost.

An entire area called Codfish Park, lying below 'Sconset between the town and the sea, contained nothing but rough fishing shacks in the old days. But as the building boom progressed and summer rentals shot up, small houses and cottages were built. A storm in December of 1992 destroyed many of them.

A year earlier a storm known on the island as the "No Name Storm," which eventually was called "The Perfect Storm" in the book and movie of that name, did tremendous damage to Old North Wharf and

Codfish Park.

flooded the streets of the lower part of town. No part of Nantucket, even on the harbor side, is immune to the forces of nature.

The most sought after land, commanding the highest prices out of town, is the high ground with water views (even distant water views). Almost all the houses erected in the nineties are sited thus. I remember, a long time ago, when a choice area called Blueberry Hill off Polpis Road, where Nantucket families had picked fruit since time-out-of-mind, was bought by some summer people who built an impressive house. Tom Giffin, then the editor of the *Nantucket Inquirer and Mirror,* wrote an editorial bemoaning the situation. He wondered if all the high ground, wherever it was on the island, would be bought up and built upon. At the time some thought him an alarmist, but his remarks turned out to be prophetic. What he worried about has happened. There is no unprotected underdeveloped high land left on the island. (Of course "high" is a relative term. Nantucket is so flat, for the most part, that even a modest elevation is significant.) Trophy houses abound, which is one of the reasons why one must go on foot, rather than driving the roads, to get a better feel for the island. From the roads you see the summer mansions on high ground to the left and to the right. On foot it is possible to discover surprising places—a ramshackle little cottage (called a "tear-down" in the real estate business) at the edge of a salt marsh, the cranberry bogs, the wild and beautiful land and water around the University of Massachusetts Field Station, or a large pond in a shallow valley in the moors. (The Field Station recently closed, making everyone both sad and nervous. The director, Wes Tiffany, was much admired and is now gone. The large spread of land is so astronomically valuable that the pressures on the university to sell it—they promise they won't—must be strong indeed.) It is a sad fact that many visitors to Nantucket do not, in fact, ever see much of what is most beautiful about the island.

⚊

RECENT TRENDS ON Nantucket bear out the observations of Thorstein Veblen, the economic thinker who, in Chapter Four of *The Theory of the Leisure Class,* first proposed the idea of "conspicuous consumption" as a driving force in human affairs. Enormous houses have sprung up like expensive mushrooms, making the old whaling days' competition on Upper Main Street look like small potatoes (to mix my metaphors). Long before the stock market began its bearish trend, the island became a status symbol much more potent than the Hamptons, or Palm Beach, or indeed anyplace on the East Coast. Seriously rich people began to make their mark as more and more young ordinary people were forced to leave the island where they were born because they could not afford to live there, because they had no future there.

An irresistible example of the degree of stratification in the society is implicit in the case of Tom Johnson, a forty-year-old ordinary Joe who got around the land and housing problem by creating a living space hidden underground on unimproved property in the woods owned by the Boy Scouts of America. Johnson, whose abode was discovered in 1999 by a deer hunter, should certainly have qualified for Eagle Scout merit badges by making, as described in *Nantucket Only Yesterday,* an "underground home . . . found to be warm and comfortable, with heating and plumbing and water and shower facilities." Johnson was of course busted by the town, but quite a few native islanders were tickled pink at the man's ingenuity. He had not needed a million or two to make his home. The story was picked up by the national press and television, and the island got a good deal of publicity, albeit a special kind.

Who will do the construction work for the conspicuous homes when the labor pool of islanders in the trades is too small to meet demand? When the cost of even temporary housing for working people is prohibitive? Off-island crews, who fly in from Hyannis and New Bedford every morning, sometimes bringing lunch, to put in their eight hours and fly back to the mainland before the sun sets. This has been going on for some time, and could only happen in a place where getting a plumber, a carpenter, a house painter can be sufficiently complex as to cause at least one rich and famous woman (who shall remain nameless) to scandalize practically everyone by offering triple time to workmen who would show up to do the work *now*, so the new house would be ready for guests in time for the start of the season. Given the high cost of skilled labor to begin with, this wretched excess indeed.

Who lives in the big houses? One day I saw a uniformed maid in a large hardware/lumber/department store called Marine Home Center holding a shopping list presumably drawn up by her employer. She wanted thirty-five plastic garment bags, forty complete sets of bed linen (from Ireland), a set of Sheffield china her mistress had previously selected, a Weber grill, and twenty lightbulbs—and put it in the black Lexus SUV outside, please. I actually overheard this, and I proceeded to have a fantasy about the people paying for it all.

Their house is on the high ground with a view of the harbor. They paid three and a half million for it, and it is the wife's job, with the help of her staff, to keep it up and running. The garden is a particular pleasure of hers, as are the relaxed lunches with friends at the Chanticleer in 'Sconset, or 21 Federal, or The Galley by the water. She has children and there is a nanny. She enjoys sailing, swimming, and horse-back riding. She keeps busy.

The husband works on Wall Street but comes up every Thursday afternoon in his co-leased private jet (forty minutes' flight time) and doesn't leave till Monday morning. On Nantucket he has paid three hundred thousand dollars for a golf club membership (I kid you not), where he plays a good game and gets a lot of business done with his peers or special guests he's brought with him from the city. In an odd way neither the husband nor the wife has much of a connection to Nantucket, which is simply the luxurious setting for their summertime activities.

I should mention that they have a cat, Ramses, upon whom they dote. At the end of the season, when they leave in a blue Ford Expedition to catch the ferry (having reserved space six months earlier), Ramses is nowhere to be found. The cat has understood the significance of all the suitcases, of the pink cat box, and has taken off into the scrub. After a good deal of discussion, the husband convinces the wife that they have no choice—they have to catch the ferry and leave Ramses behind. They will alert the care-taker to keep an eye out for the animal. Quite a few cats suffer this fate every year.

Ramses undergoes some severe life-style changes,

by the way. From Tender Vittles, his diet changes, first to frogs, garter snakes, and small birds, but eventually, as the cat becomes feral and grows to seventeen pounds, to squirrels, pheasants, and rabbits. Feral cats are considered a dangerous nuisance by islanders, and they are legally shot and killed by the sometime game warden, deer hunters, and duck hunters. Ramses is one of ninety cats so dispatched that particular winter. It is, in fact, the caretaker who finishes him off with his shotgun, while out flushing game birds.

I LOVE AIRPORT NOISE

It's true. There's an awful lot more than there used to be. Jets and props all day long.

PIPING PLOVERS TASTE LIKE CHICKEN

In protest to closing four wheel-drive access to Great Point because the birds nested in the tire tracks.

20 IS PLENTY IN 'SCONSET

Twenty miles per hour. Good advice because the streets are narrow, and many of the cottages are inches away from the berm. Some natives change the sticker with Magic Markers to read:

80 IS PLENTY IN 'SCONSET

Since the town is almost completely summer people. (Often spotted behind a beer and shots bar called the Chicken Box.)

The Pace Quickens

SOMETIME IN THE SEVENTIES I HAD A TALK with a local minister about the island. He was worried about a lot of things, but most particularly about the laundering of drug money in Nantucket real estate. He did not tell me his sources of information, nor did he mention any names, but it seemed to me, in that age of cocaine, to be quite possible. In fact it was not long after our talk that a guy I knew—I'll call him Swifty—was arrested (and not by local law enforcement) for trafficking heroin. Swifty had a T-shirt store downtown which provided a light rinse for his ill-gotten gains, which were finally laundered in the purchase of an expensive cottage in 'Sconset. The cottage was confiscated and Swifty went to jail, but he'd come close to getting away with it. Nantucket operated on money from off island, and no one seemed to worry too much about where the money came from. (Heroin continues to be a problem even today. There seems to be something about island life—not just on Nantucket—that makes people susceptible to alcohol and drugs. The per capita consumption of booze on Nantucket is the highest in the state. Heroin users on the island are not like users in the cities. They are, for the most part, working men, often with families, and not easily spotted by straight people. I have known two men from the trades who have died of drug overdoses, for instance, and I was truly surprised in both instances.)

The minister was also worried that the town was losing its soul, so to speak, as more money and more houses and more people became more important than "the courtesy and manners that are critical to the texture of life in a small town," as David Halberstam, a longtime summer resident, phrased it in *Town and Country.* The center could not hold, said the minister, as the island lost its identity even to its own sons and daughters.

Rich men have affected the island in many ways for many years, and quite often to the good. Old money has protected 'Sconset, for instance—well-to-do summer residents closing ranks to protect the village. Islanders remember Roy Larsen with fondness (at least those interested in conservation and preservation), for starting the Conservation Foundation and for donating large parcels of open land. A far-seeing gentleman, to be sure.

At the risk of appearing snobbish, I cannot help but compare the character of the philanthropists of the sixties and seventies, even of the eighties, with some of those of the nineties and the aught. Dennis Kozlowski, for example, under indictment for milking $600 million (along with two other men) from Tyco while he was CEO. There is a mural in the anteroom of the ER at Nantucket Cottage Hospital celebrating Kozlowski, his boat, and his status as angel. No one worried about where the money came from. No one probably knew the man well enough to be able to foresee what would come out in the criminal investigation—that, even in small matters, he spent crassly: $2,900 for hangers, $6,300 for a sewing kit, $15,000 for an umbrella stand, $17,000 for an antique toilet kit, $6,000 for a shower curtain, and so on. Kozlowski apparently took Nantucket more seriously than the couple with the cat. He wanted to buy his way in through civic good works, through giving money away. He succeeded, at least until the year 2002 when the Enron, Tyco, and other scandals finally broke. But did he really? Or was David Halberstam correct when he observed, "Many of the true pleasures of Nantucket are not easily gained and cannot be purchased on demand . . . they have to be like

everything else in life, earned." It's hard to imagine
that Mr. Kozlowski would understand the true pleasures Halberstam refers to.

⟐

PEOPLE CONSIDERING A visit to Nantucket should
know that they are welcome, that they are needed,
truth be told. A long time ago when the year-round
population was three and a half thousand, the island
lived off a ten-week summer season. But now the
population is approaching ten thousand, and everything possible is being done to make the season start
earlier and last longer.

There has been a pattern in many of these efforts.
Start with a local initiative, however small, expand it,
and advertise it. A well-known force in the Garden
Club, Mrs. MacAusland was perhaps inspired by Lady-
bird Johnson's Beautify America campaign when she
and her cohorts started planting daffodil bulbs at the
edges of roads, in the rotary, along the bike paths and
other strategic spots. They planted thousands and
thousands of bulbs over the years, and the results were
spectacular. From this emerged Daffodil Weekend in
April, which attracts many visitors from America, including various off-island garden clubs, and those
who simply need an excuse to come over for a visit.
This despite the fact that April can be a cruel month

on Nantucket. April 2002 was particularly so when a storm trapped a lot of visitors who wound up spending the night in the high school gymnasium. A celebratory mood prevailed, apparently.

In May, there is the Wine Festival, started by Denis Toner, a local sommelier, more or less for his friends and colleagues. It grew beyond his imaginings, moving from his house to larger venues, most recently the White Elephant Hotel, a snazzy environment if there ever was one. Today famous chefs from New York, France, and other culinary centers fly up and guest-cook at local restaurants. Wine merchants, collectors, and aficionados come from the East Coast along with media people to cover the action. It has become a very big deal indeed.

In June there is the film festival, started by a local brother and sister team, both young, which has grown in stature and importance every year. The first East Coast screening of *The Full Monty* occurred at the Nantucket Film Festival, along with other independently produced movies.

There is the Island Jazz and Folk Festival, the Cranberry Festival, and the Nectar Fest, this last started by two young guys, Tom First and Tom Scott, who spent the winter of 1990 making and bottling fruit drinks, which they sold from a boat to the yachting crowd in the jam-packed harbor and marina the next summer. Their business, Nantucket Nectars,

Snow on Main Street.

expanded, went national, and was worth $35 million by 1996, when they sold it to Ocean Spray. The Nectar Fest involves music, of course, and fund-raising for island causes.

❦

A CLOSE LOOK AT THE annual Christmas Stroll reveals a good deal about the recent history of Nantucket.

I remember the first Stroll, back in the seventies, when Maggie and I lived on the island year-round. We knew a number of people who worked in the shops, or ran them (paying high rent to Sherburne), who were concerned about locals going to the strip malls of Hyannis to do their Christmas shopping at the franchise retailers. The Nantucket markup was built so deeply into the system that even with the best will in the world, local retailers could not avoid it. So it began as a small-scale local initiative to encourage locals to buy on-island. Main Street was lined with miniature Christmas trees strung with lights and decorations. The shops stayed open late, doorways and windows spilling light, welcoming people inside for punch, canapés, and cookies, or shots and beers on the sly for special friends. (I found myself with a distinct buzz on before I was halfway up the street.) A nice, warm holiday party, in which one knew everybody in the shops and on the sidewalks. It was fun. A sense of community prevailed, and from a business point of view it made sense—some dollars stayed on the island that might otherwise have left.

The goals changed gradually, as the Chamber of Commerce and the tourist industry advertised the Stroll, giving an old-fashioned small-town image, a kind of false nostalgic glow.

It was marketed, in other words, in order to attract visitors. People began to fly in, or take the ferry (having arranged accommodations at a hotel or a bed-and-breakfast), in order to take the Stroll and do some shopping. The number of visitors increased as the island's status increased, and, paradoxically, as the shops became more luxe and more expensive: jewelry, $800 cashmere sweaters, lightship baskets decorated with scrimshaw, fancy housewares, antiques, gee-gaws, and the like. The original idea turned upside-down because the islanders could no longer afford the shops at all. The question was no longer the Nantucket markup, it was what might be called the Veblenization of Main Street.

It did not seem to matter that visitors might find themselves, as they once did, socked in by weather. They came anyway. Recently fifteen thousand people came for the Stroll. One and a half times the population, in other words. Change happens, shrug the locals, and they ought to know.

So Much to Do

FAMILIES THINKING OF RENTING A HOUSE for the summer should be aware that Nantucket is nothing less than a paradise for children. My three sons (now age forty, thirty-eight, and sixteen) all had unconscionable amounts of fun—and this is one area where the island is even better now than it was when my oldest were kids.

Let's start with small kids. What does one do with them? All of my kids picked blackberries along the sides of the long driveway leading to our house. (How do you make a driveway? You simply drive over the same track, time after time, and you wind up with a dirt road, with grass in the raised center strip. Over the years the road sinks down, and you get puddles when it rains.) For all of my kids, and for Jonathan and Nicholas, my three-year-old twin grandchildren, picking berries was the first foray into the outside world of the island.

Everyone's first beach experience was on the shore of Quidnet Pond, where only thirty yards of dunes separate the waters of the open harbor from the intimate pond, always calm whatever the weather. Quidnet is a cluster of houses—most of them modest old-money summer homes—far enough away from everything to be a sort of secret, special place. Small children play in the sand, wade in the water, and make up games. Sometimes a mom throws a tennis ball for her pooch (quite often a Labrador) to retrieve. Sometimes a dad will fly a kite, or shmooze with other dads, all the while keeping an eye on the water. The kids are totally absorbed with one another, and it's rare to see them fuss.

What youngster could pass up throwing bread into the pond off Polpis Road near Hollywood Farm (no longer a farm—although once what is called an old lady's farm where my first wife and I would buy baby vegetables and really splendid watermelon pickles made by Mrs. Maglathlin, the owner) in order to see the snapping turtles rise to the surface?

And what about hermit crabs at the Brant Point breakwater? The sight of these prehistoric life forms seems specially thrilling to the young. As the kids grow a bit older they might go out to Madaket Bridge and throw chicken legs, tied with a long string, into the water to catch crabs. Again the fascination of primitive life forms, spiced by the aura of danger. Watch those claws!

The kids discover the joys of clamming and of the fact that you can bring something back for dinner even if you're only seven years old, let's say. We always went out to a tidal flat near the entrance to Polpis Harbor in our boat, with the dog. Maggie and I might swim while Tim, my youngest, went off with a bucket for an hour. We could see him in the distance, hunkered down, his small form bright in the stark sunlight, elbows akimbo, digging with purpose. Or on a foggy day, he would simply disappear as the sound of buoy bells rang muffled in the air. We call it Tim's Point, and we go there often.

There are any number of children's groups, from the Wee Whalers, a day-care operation, to the more upscale Maria Mitchell Association's nature group with visits to interesting sites around the island—places like Gibbs Pond, hidden away in the moors, or various marshlands. A group called Strong Wings provides a kind of outward-bound experience, encouraging kids to test physical and mental limits. (Many children's groups—more than one—visit a conservation holding in the forest next to our house. We can hear their voices from our vantage point on the rear deck, and they sometimes cross over into our little forest, or so it sounds.) Dozens of play groups feature different kinds of activities. Even the Nantucket Island School of Design and the Arts, NISDA, has programs for children.

When it rains there is a splendid children's wing in the Atheneum, in the town library, with readings, singing, and various games. The hall above the main library was the site for many famous lectures in the nineteenth century. The lectures and readings for adults continue on, but the library has recently shown a gradual but definite tilt toward children—who sometimes spill out into the adjacent park to roll in the grass or climb the trees.

The recent introduction of public transport, buses on a regular schedule, has opened things up for older children, who can go into town whenever they want to eat pizza, get ice cream on old South Wharf, or pick up a video to take back home. Parents need not worry because the island is safe. Kids can go anywhere, and they do, enjoying a kind of independence no longer possible on the mainland.

Boat rides around the harbor are always fun, and somebody's dad seems always to suggest a trip out to Tuckernuck, where on the way one sees seals basking in the sun on Esther Island, black eyes flashing above their whiskers. The south shore of Tuckernuck is a splendid place to fish for striped bass and bluefish. The island used to be half deserted, and I can remember coming over in Walter Barrett's boat as he delivered mail and groceries to the tiny pier. As soon as one stepped on land a hundred seagulls would begin to track from the air, gradually coming closer, diving down like creatures in a Hitchcock film. A bit scary, always, as I walked across the sandy ground to the old LaFarge compound, where I had friends. (In fact my first wife contracted hepatitis there, eating shellfish from the inlet.) Nowadays there are quite a few houses and the land is expensive, if any is available. The fishing is still superb, either from the shore into the surf, or from a boat outside, casting back into the surf (à la the late Bob "Stinky" Francis, a local who took out fishing parties for a fee—or for no charge if you got skunked).

There is the Dreamland Theater, where the audience is less inhibited than at any other movie theater I know. The big summer movies are always packed with kids laughing, hissing, and booing like Italian opera fans. I saw *Psycho* at the Dreamland when it was first released, and will never forget the shocked, almost dazed look on people's faces as we emerged, many of us going directly to Gwen Gaillard's Opera House for a stiff drink.

There is also the tiny Gaslight Theater, but for kids the best movie venue is probably the old hall in 'Sconset, where the audience sits on folding chairs and everybody knows everybody else. A true summertime feeling, not much different than it was thirty or forty years ago. As I mentioned before, 'Sconset has worked hard to maintain its traditions.

Teenagers do not need cars (although many of them seem to have the use of them) because they can bike anywhere on the extensive network of bike paths or take the bus. They go to the South Shore with Boogie boards or surfboards, having called the hot line for an up-to-the-minute description of the size of the waves. They can spend a long time—all day—at Cisco or Nobadeer beaches knowing they can get hot dogs and ice cream from the truck or from the hip vendor who uses an old motorcycle with a dry-ice sidecar.

Beach parties seem to occur quite often in the evenings, and teenagers get to know each other, sometimes very well indeed, and perhaps quaff an illicit beer or two before the recently imposed ten-thirty party curfew. The cops, who show up on dune buggies, are invariably polite and understanding, some of them not much older than the kids. They are able to blend in, sort of, standing around the bonfires with everybody else.

All sorts of activities are available. At sixteen, Tim rides horseback with his pal Seth in the shallows of Polpis Harbor or on Quaise Pastures. He plays tennis in 'Sconset (and works at the club desk scheduling games for people), jogs to Altar Rock, practices stick-shifting on isolated dirt roads, or goes into town for a pizza on our old fifty-horsepower duck boat. The day is not long enough for him and his buddies. They love the island with a passion and never seem to take it for granted.

Boats

A s we had Third World Softball, we also had the more amorphous Third World Yacht Club. The first members being myself and John Krebs, a pal who keeps his inflatable on my point since he does not have access to the water from his property. I started with an old scallop boat, and actually tried to earn some money scalloping with my friend Phil.

We worked the harbor, and work it surely was. Winter. Socks, and then wool socks for a second layer. Rubber boots that almost reached your knees. Long underwear, jeans and wool shirts, a heavy sweater and full weather slicks. Workman's gloves. We would putt-putt through Polpis Harbor out into Nantucket Harbor proper, cutting the engine when we reached a likely spot, which meant a smooth rock-free bottom where scallops rest in the eel grass. Chain-link dredges on iron frames are tossed overboard, the engine is started, and the ropes begin to feed out. When the dredges fall into the proper staggered pattern, a bit more power is coaxed from the outboard engine and the dredges are pulled twenty-five yards or more. The outboard is placed in neutral, and the outboard "donkey engine" (scavenged from a lawn mower) is cranked up, its drum extension turning, waiting for the rope which gets wrapped around the drum in such a way that the dredges, one by one, are pulled in.

There is a culling board athwart the center of the boat. The most dangerous part of the operation is leaning over the side and manhandling the dredge, now full, weighing close to a hundred pounds, up onto the culling board to spill out crabs, seaweed, eel grass, gunk, and, one hopes, scallops. It is at the precise moment of pulling up the dredge that you can slip and fall overboard. With the boots, heavy clothing, and slickers, drowning is a certainty without quick help from one's partner.

The scallops are picked out of the mess on the culling board, the year-old ones (you can tell by the rings) thrown back into the water along with the slightly slimy vegetation. Then the dredges are thrown over and another run commences.

I gave it up one foggy day when I was out alone. I was getting scallops, but at one point I almost lost my balance. I was simply not strong enough to pull up the dredges smoothly, and I had a sudden flash of my vulnerability. I decided then and there to give up scalloping, and in fact never attempted it again. (Phil was also ready to throw in the towel.) Instead I used the boat to go fishing when the weather was warm and the sun shone.

During the summer I worked at night, playing jazz, or now and then doing magazine pieces in the daytime. I found myself spending more and more time fishing, not for money, but because I liked it.

Island wisdom had it that Polpis Harbor held so few fish that working it would be a waste of time. I was absurdly pleased with myself to prove otherwise. I fished with a surf rod, standing on the culling board, and I discovered that Polaroid sunglasses allowed me to see into the water to a depth of four or five feet. Weeks of moving from spot to spot, throwing anchor and casting the shiny drail, allowed me over time to discover that striped bass, and the occasional bluefish, entered and exited the harbor along specific channels, and that even at the southern end they moved along certain pathways. I could see them—dark, fast-moving shadows streaking along over the sandy bottom—and I learned how to cast in front of them. The excitement attendant to a strike, the sudden pull, the fish often leaping up into the air, never failed to thrill me, no matter how many fish I caught.

The sought-after fish is the striped bass—mild, sweet, and easy to cook. Bluefish, much more com-

mon in Nantucket waters, are oily, with a strong fishy
flavor, and make a fine pâté (an island specialty). They
can be broiled, soaked in gin, and touched with a lit
match to lift out some of the oil, as the late Robert
Benchley used to do it, to good effect.

There is a curious fact associated with bluefish.
Wauwinet, Quaise, Shawkemo, Polpis, Quidnet, Madaket, Coatue, etc., are all Anglicized Indian names.
Indians were the first people on the island, as far back
as circa 300 A.D., the carbon date for some deer bone
tools dug out of the earth.

Stone arrowheads and blades can be found all over
the island by the trained eye. (The Unitarian minister
has more than once plucked up an arrowhead from
my driveway, despite my having searched carefully
and finding nothing. He has a wonderful collection.)
The Indians died out, and when the last one expired,
the bluefish disappeared. The oral history connects the
two events. For seventy-five years not a single bluefish
was caught. These days it is not uncommon to see
small boats come in with big catches, the fish having
returned even if the Indians did not.

A small cycle occurred in Polpis Harbor, where
twenty-five years ago there were so many blue shell
crabs scuttling around that I could pole net twenty or
thirty in an hour. They disappeared for quite some
time, but show signs of coming back.

I remember one morning in the early seventies

when I was anchored in a particularly good position on the south side of Second Point, where the channel the fish used was narrow and well defined. My reel was snarled and I sat down and fixed it. When I looked up I saw two friends, who'd heard that I was catching fish, in a rowboat fishing on the other side of the point. We waved to each other and I thought of telling them to come over, but some atavistic fisher/hunter reflex kept me silent. It was (at that time) *my* harbor, after all. So Alan and Twig had to sit in their boat, catching nothing, and watch me pull in three nice-sized bass in perhaps twenty casts. Later, I told them during a beery dart game about the channels, but they never came back. It was a long haul from town, in any case.

I really didn't have enough money to maintain *Que Blahmo* properly, but I was determined to keep it. Mooring was a problem, since I did not have a mushroom (as they called it). I tied cement blocks (no good) and finally a heavy iron engine stand, which seemed to work. In the morning I could look out my window while eating breakfast and see the heavy, green, funky boat bobbing in the water.

Eventually there was a gale, from the south, and the boat pulled the engine stand out of the mud and dragged it up harbor, where *Que Blahmo* finally sank, fifty-horse Evinrude and all. Here one moment, totally gone the next.

I should have gotten the message and washed my hands of the whole business, but I didn't. With the kind of stubbornness that can affect you when you're close to broke, I insisted on keeping up my fishing life-style, not falling back, as it were. I began to haunt the shipyard out in Madaket, finally acting when an inexpensive used boat became available. I got it cheap because it was aluminum, and riveted hulls were definitely out of favor on Nantucket. It was an old black Starcraft from the fifties, with red vinyl seats, a padded dash, and a windshield—so retro I had to have it. No more standing on the culling board, but I already knew where the channels were, so it didn't matter. I called it *Elvis,* and it was fast enough so I could take my boys water skiing, which they loved for a couple of years and then mysteriously lost interest. I had gotten a mushroom this time, but stupidly overlooked the proper clasps, knots, and other paraphernalia with which the rope from the boat is attached to the mooring. Simple ignorance. One afternoon, during a hurricane, I stood at the rain-streaked window thinking I should have beached the boat, only to see a granny knot fail and the boat sail away up harbor with the wind.

I ran down to the water, and then along the shore as the boat lurched along in the angry water to come to rest in the shallows of the long spit of land separating the north end of Polpis Harbor from Nantucket

Harbor proper. The wind was fearsome—seventy to eighty miles an hour, I would later learn—but as I saw waves breaking over the stern of the boat I jumped into the waist-high water and got behind it, hoping to save the engine. As I struggled (ineffectively) to lift the stern, a sudden gust took the glasses off my head. In a surreal moment I watched them fly up into the air, way up, and disappear over the spit, higher and higher, smaller and smaller, until I couldn't see them anymore. The boat swamped and the engine was lost. Eventually the wind actually blew the boat over and upside-down, bending the windshield beyond repair. *Elvis* was trashed out, and, brokenhearted, I would eventually give the hull away.

Boats are more heartbreak and worry than they are a joy. Something always seems to go wrong. An engine briefly catches on fire on the way to Coatue. The battery dies for no apparent reason. The draining hole stopper dries out and springs a leak. I don't know how many mornings I would come down to the window half expecting the boat to have disappeared, then relieved that it had not, but still nervous enough to worry if the stern might not be riding a bit heavy in the water. I knew I wasn't the only one to feel anxiety. My good friend David Halberstam had a Boston Whaler for a while, from which we fished out in the ocean, but he finally gave it up. "Marine engines," he said. "The tolerances are like airplane engines, so

Gracie and Maggie.

they're expensive, but they keep conking out anyway."
For many years now he has glided through the harbor
in his racing scull, keeping fit while enjoying the
water.

The fact is, once you've tooled around in Nantucket waters, once you see the island from that vantage point, you can't easily give it up entirely. It
becomes essential that you have a way to go over to
Coatue for private skinny-dipping, or into town via
the harbor to see the hundreds of yachts moored there
or tied up at the docks. In recent years there seem to

be more and more really big yachts, sometimes with helicopters tied down on deck. Frank Sinatra sailed in one day, a young woman dressed in white playing a flute in the bow as they docked. The boat was enormous, of course.

And there are more intimate pleasures—bird watching from a kayak small enough to let you navigate up a stream, and then back down to, for instance, Polpis Harbor, where Maggie likes to paddle along with our dog Gracie shadowing her.

THE YEARS PASSED, during which I began teaching at the University of Iowa and M.I.T. My financial situation improved markedly, and I started haunting Madaket Marine again. And so I came by the boat we have today, a seventeen-foot Chincoteegue brought up from the Chesapeake (it's a duck boat) by a member of the Dupont family who fell too ill to use it. We named it *Buzz Cut,* and we're now on the second engine.

During the season a lot of people live on their boats, and the harbor fills up. The launch is in continuous operation taking people to and from the wharf. I should mention the Nantucket Lightship (a floating lighthouse), which was decommissioned years

Frank and engine.

ago, spent time in various mainland harbors, and was finally brought back to Nantucket by someone who bought it on eBay. Fitted out for landlubbers, it can be rented, and lived in, for fourteen thousand dollars a week.

Slow Down! You're Already on Nantucket

Periodically an idea comes up in one town meeting or the other: a scheme to control the number of automobiles coming onto the island. Nothing changes, however. Even limits that seem sensible, say, two or three cars per household, never get implemented. As cars rule America, cars rule Nantucket. The summer traffic in town is so intense it has affected the way the island has grown. More and more facilities, from the supermarket to an ancillary post office, are located in what is now the outskirts of town. Small clusters of retailers, most of them pretty fancy, seem to have sprung up everywhere. Niche restaurants abound, every one with a parking lot. Downyflake Doughnuts, where working people and families can get lunch at reasonable prices, is out of town. (A hallowed institution, by the way, and well worth a visit, even at six-thirty in the morning.)

FRANK CONROY

I am on the island as I write this. I went into town at 11:30 this morning with a few errands to do, using a system that works well enough to allow me to do everything in two and a half hours.

First you must plan. The mail. (And thereby hangs a tale. We've had a post office box for thirty-five years, which we are loath to give up because there is a six-year waiting list to get one. We could use a mailbox at the end of our driveway, of course, but we don't. The post office identifies us as long-term Nantucketers, and I admit we are irrationally proud of that fact.)

A slice of pizza and a Nantucket Nectars lemonade from the Steamship Wharf would be nice. Pick up an orange juice machine at the Marine Home Center (housewares section). Croissants. The *New York Times*. Two dust masks.

Ordinarily one would do it by the map, going from one place to the next, but there is a better way.

The system involves going into the clotted heart of town to check out the post office first. Today there were no parking places within two blocks so I didn't stop, but moved slowly through the side streets to come out at the pizza place. There were no spaces there either, but I knew I could park on the road the trucks use to get on the ferry if I left my lights flashing as I dashed across the street. (The pizza was good. The best on the island, in fact. I ate in the car.)

Then back to the post office, and this time a car pulls out of a space just as I arrive, so I park, get the mail (and the *New York Times* from The Hub), and continue on my way. Halfway out of town I stop at the Nantucket Bakery for croissants. As I continue homeward I stop at the Marine Home Center (parking lot) for the juicer, Island Lumber (parking lot) for the dust masks, and so back home.

Remain flexible, the system says. Never stop unless a car pulls out of a parking place, or you are out of town. Drive around the block. Breathe deeply. Play soothing music on the radio. Smile.

The island is proud that there are no traffic lights anywhere. And this is as irrational as keeping a post office box. There are at least four complicated intersections everyone knows should have traffic lights, both for safety and to speed things up. Everyone also knows it won't happen in the foreseeable future.

Traffic is a problem in a lot of places, but the combination of Nantucket's narrow streets and the presence of Hummers, Expeditions, and other oversized vehicles (Veblen!) makes things particularly tough. The bicycle paths, and the introduction of public transport, have helped a bit, but more and more cars seem to come each summer, with no signs of slowing down.

ACK

Not a bumper sticker, but a decal spelling out the
code for Nantucket airport. A favorite of summer
people rather than natives.

ACK NICELY

A gentle warning to the visitors

NATIVE

And proud of it. Although a lot of people
have been forced out, many have stayed,
toughing out the high cost of living.

NATIVE.
AN ENDANGERED SPECIES

A Certain Romance

THE *NEW YORK TIMES* REPORTS ON THE popularity of what it calls "destination weddings," and Nantucket turns out to be a prime example. The Chamber of Commerce has an information clearing house, listing churches, caterers, photographers, musicians, tent rentals, bartenders, and everything else that might be needed. (A good friend of ours, Mary Keller—she of the chador—plays her harp at such events and earns a significant part of her income thus.) It is not that hard to understand why people might want to be married on Nantucket. A certain romance attends to crossing thirty miles of ocean to arrive at a beautiful, historic, unique, and high-status island. Some marry in churches, others on the beach, or in a garden, or even in the moors. For all of them, one surmises, the event and the memory of the event are framed by the Nantucket atmosphere, which, like sense memories of food or the scent of flowers, is exceedingly difficult to capture in words while remaining quite vivid in memory. In many ways the island is a splendid place to get married. People smile when they see a wedding, as if the celebration is communal, and of course, most essentially, it is.

I've described elsewhere how I met my wife on Nantucket more than thirty years ago. She was hitchhiking because her car had a dead battery, and in accordance with the winter rules, I picked her up. We hit it off immediately and were married in the Episcopal church a year or so later. Maggie's mother and her large network of Boston pals stayed at the Jared Coffin House and had a good time, watching the Kentucky Derby at the reception, cocktails aloft.

Places can insinuate themselves into your very soul if you have lived and grown there. I cannot separate my love for Maggie from my love for the island, for instance. There are overlaps. (And in a totally different way I love our ten-months-a-year home in Iowa City, where I wrote two books and learned how to teach.)

〰

I WORRY THAT I haven't done Nantucket justice in these pages. It has a special feeling, a special aspect unlike any other place I've been. (An English village in which I lived years ago. Visits to London, Paris,

Moscow, St. Petersburg, Budapest, Portugal, Spain, Mexico, and the Caribbean, to name a few. Each had a flavor, of course, but none as powerful to me as the faraway island.)

My second son met his wife on Nantucket. She was an Irish girl who'd come over for a summer job, and she wound up staying. They married on Nantucket and their son, Liam Wainwright Conroy, was born on Nantucket. There is a brick with his name on it on a special wall in the hospital. A wall, as they call it, of Native Born. So my grandson discovered Nantucket even earlier than I did, as I stood on the bow of that ship watching the boys dive for coins so long ago.

Two summers ago Julia, my daughter-in-law, was walking on the 'Sconset beach. The water was calm and she took off her shoes to wade. After a while she felt something on her ankle, reached down and retrieved a one-hundred-dollar bill. She spotted another one close by, drifting like seaweed, and kept searching for a while until it was clear there weren't any more. Probably someone had gone swimming with the money in his bathing suit with the pocket unbuttoned.

I was reminded yet again of the boys diving for coins, and of the passage of time. We live and the world changes around us, slowly, to be sure, but every now and then something happens, some unusual occurrence that stands like a signpost, a marker of the relentless passage of time which no one, and no place, can escape.

Sources

I'VE USED SEVERAL BOOKS. MOST IMPORTANT was Robert F. Mooney's excellent source book, *Nantucket Only Yesterday*, Wesco Publishing, 2000. Also helpful were *Nantucket, The Last 100 Years*, compiled and edited by John Stanton, published by the Inquirer and Mirror Press, 2001; *We Are Nantucket*, edited by Brian L.P. Zevnik, Wellington Press, 2002; and *Nantucket in the Nineteenth Century*, Clay Lancaster, Dover Publications Inc., 1979. Also, *Celestial Messengers*, a play by Maggie Conroy. My thanks to the *Inquirer and Mirror*, the Nantucket Historical Association, and the Nantucket Chamber of Commerce. My debt to all of these good people is large.

About the Author

FRANK CONROY is the longtime director of the prestigious Iowa Writers' Workshop. He is the author of *Stop-Time, Midair, Body & Soul,* and *Dogs Bark, but the Caravan Rolls On.*